BREAKING THE

FEAR

BARRIER

HOW FEAR DESTROYS COMPANIES FROM THE
INSIDE OUT AND WHAT TO DO ABOUT IT

TOM RIEGER

GALLUP PRESS
1251 Avenue of the Americas
23rd Floor
New York, NY 10020

Library of Congress Control Number: 2011923495
ISBN: 978-1-59562-054-5

First Printing: 2011
10 9 8 7 6 5 4 3 2 1

FOR DANA AND DEVIN

TABLE OF CONTENTS

INTRODUCTION 1

GLOSSARY 5

Chapter One: FEAR OF LOSS 7

    Joe's Fall From Grace 8

Chapter Two: PAROCHIALISM 21

Chapter Three: TERRITORIALISM 31

Chapter Four: EMPIRE BUILDING 43

Chapter Five: THE COST OF FEAR 49

Chapter Six: OVERCOMING PAROCHIALISM 57

Chapter Seven: OVERCOMING TERRITORIALISM 73

Chapter Eight: OVERCOMING EMPIRE BUILDING 87

Chapter Nine: COURAGE ENABLERS 99

Chapter Ten: BEWARE OF COURAGE KILLERS 111

Chapter Eleven: THE LEADERSHIP IMPERATIVE 121

Chapter Twelve: THE FEARLESS COMPANY 131

    Joe's Redemption... 134

ACKNOWLEDGEMENTS.................................. 143

REFERENCES 145

INTRODUCTION

Several years ago, as part of my consulting work with Gallup, I had the opportunity to take a close look at about a dozen organizations that had, in their own words, "become stuck." In one case, turnover spiked and would not come down. Another company was able to increase its customer loyalty in every location but one, which seemed to be repelling customers. The specifics of each situation varied, but the basic story was the same: Strategically, these companies appeared to be doing the right things and were giving workgroups and teams what they needed, but none of that seemed to matter. Something was getting in the way. Something was acting as a barrier.

So along with a hand-picked team of consultants, I got to work to see what was holding these companies back. Armed with all of the latest theories, case studies, academic papers, and journal articles, we dove right in. We looked at policies and procedures. We examined performance management systems and organizational charts. We studied every relevant aspect of every job — recruiting, hiring, training, discipline, advancement, attrition — you name it. We scrutinized everything we could get our hands on.

Very quickly, however, it became painfully obvious that all of the textbook theories about what might be holding these companies back were dead wrong. So we started from scratch and talked to people at every workgroup level, from the C-suite to the front line to the graveyard shift.

What we learned was that there were some subtle common problems eating away at the very fabric of these organizations. It didn't matter if it was a call center, a manufacturing plant, a car dealership, a bank, a sales organization, a hospital, or a retail outlet. It became quickly apparent that no matter what country, level, function, or industry, similar issues were causing the problems.

It was as if we were hearing the same story again and again. The language may have been different, but the basic lesson was the same: Fear destroys companies. More specifically, fear leads companies to destroy themselves. It happens quietly and subtly. But over time, as these businesses (and countless others we have studied since) became more complex, fear of loss led to bureaucracy, inefficiency, low morale, and ultimately, failure.

I need to make an important distinction here: Not all fear is bad. Feeling pressure to perform and being held accountable for goals is not harmful. It's necessary. But when people fear losing respect, losing power, not getting a bonus, or *losing something* they feel entitled to, they can feel compelled to create walls. While those walls may shelter one person or group, they leave others out in the cold.

I saw firsthand how easy it is for fear to crush people and break their spirits and how quickly barriers can kill enthusiasm and energy. I watched walls make life a lot easier for a small part of an organization while undermining the rest of the company. I saw short-term, quick-fix decisions that guaranteed long-term failure and how fear crippled any hope of sustained success. I saw organization after organization build seemingly impenetrable pyramids of bureaucracy, where the barriers put up by one group out of fear compelled others to create barriers of their own.

Fortunately, I also saw that because these barriers were created internally, they could be torn down internally. Over time, in organizations that dealt with barriers and fear properly, the changes were nothing less than extraordinary: Service rankings changed from worst to first, turnover dropped dramatically, sales increased, and morale skyrocketed.

In the aftermath of the Great Recession, while organizations are still dealing with widespread loss and fear, it's easy for them to give up hope that they can get back that edge, that swagger, and that fierce pride that drove success in the past. But it's still out there. That hope still lives inside every employee, manager, and leader. To unleash that hope, organizations must utterly destroy the fear barrier. The first step is to understand how fear works and how barriers are constructed and sustained so that the underlying root causes can be destroyed one by one. The second step is to create an environment where courageous behavior can flourish and thrive.

Breaking the Fear Barrier is the result of what my team and I saw, what we learned, and what we have since found to be true in virtually every organization we have studied. It shows how and why fear destroys success and demonstrates how to transform a fear-plagued, barrier-ridden organization into one that is fearless and unstoppable. This is a difficult journey but one that can mean the difference between success and utter failure, between dreams realized and hopes dashed. It is a journey we can't afford *not* to take.

GLOSSARY

Barrier: A policy, practice, or behavior that limits the success of an individual, group, or organization.

Empire building: Attempts to assert control over people, functions, or resources in an effort to regain or enhance self-sufficiency.

Moral courage: Behavior or actions that involve some element of effort or risk that are designed to promote a larger purpose or greater good.

Parochialism: A tendency to force others to view the world from only one perspective or through a narrow filter, when local needs and goals are viewed as more important than broader objectives and outcomes.

Territorialism: Hoarding or micromanaging internal headcount, resources, or decision authority in an effort to maintain control.

Vital courage: Behavior or actions that involve some element of effort or risk that are designed to ensure survival or otherwise lead to tangible and meaningful personal gain or improvement.

Chapter One:
FEAR OF LOSS

In his 1985 State of the Union address, Ronald Reagan said, "There are no constraints on the human mind, no walls around the human spirit, no barriers to our progress except those we ourselves erect."

So why do we do it? Why do so many organizations plague themselves with barrier after barrier and create cumbersome, lumbering bureaucracies that can't quickly respond to market changes or new conditions? By creating internal barriers, countless organizations damage themselves with red tape, interdepartmental conflict, inefficient processes, restrictive policies, or too much or too little information.

Consider the plight of Joe, whose story is based on actual people and events.

JOE'S FALL FROM GRACE

3:00 a.m.

Joe looked over at the clock.

"I wish I could sleep," he muttered to himself.

Joe didn't know what was worse: lying in bed stressed out over what happened at work yesterday or having to get up and face another day. He wondered yet again how things got so bad so fast.

When Joe first joined his company, the world was full of promise. His wife and daughter were so proud. His family had given up so much for him to be able to finish his degree. When this new customer service manager job came his way, it was a dream come true. It was worth everything they'd sacrificed, or so it seemed.

During his interviews, Joe was full of new ideas and excited about the challenge of transforming his new company's customer service department from its industry-worst position to the cornerstone of the company's success. His passion, creativity, and desire to make things better were what gave him the edge over the other candidates, he was told. Plus, he had worked in a call center when he was in college and knew the industry.

As he left for work on his first day, Joe could see his family beaming. He could barely contain his excitement about having a chance to apply his ideas. He read everything he could get his hands on, carefully studied best practices in the industry, and took detailed notes every time he had a good service experience anywhere. He couldn't wait to jump in. "I am really going to make a difference," he thought to himself as he got in the car.

When Joe arrived at work, Mary, the director of customer service, greeted him at the door. "I've arranged for a meeting with your team to help them get to know you. It starts at 10:00, which should give you enough time to fill out your paperwork with HR and find your way around. Let me know what else I can do to help. We'll talk toward the end of the day."

"Thanks, Mary!" said Joe. "I am really looking forward to working together."

At 10:00, eager to make a good impression, Joe entered the conference room. His staff consisted of six team leaders, each of whom supervised between 10 and 12 customer service representatives. The first thing Joe noticed was the heavy silence in the room. A few people tried to smile and mutter a greeting. It was not quite what he expected.

Shrugging off the cool reception, Joe went around the room to get to know each person. Then he started to share his vision that nothing was more important than engaged employees helping make customers for life. He told his staff that they'd fight for change together and how this group would take the lead in transforming the organization. He was fired up and on a roll. But no one made a single comment or even asked a question. Joe found it a bit unsettling that the only responses he got were exchanges of raised eyebrows and wide-eyed looks between a few of the team leaders. As the weeks wore on, Joe began to understand why.

His first inkling of what was to come arrived with some paperwork a few weeks later. Like any other call center, all calls were recorded. Every month, the quality assurance department, or QA, randomly selected and scored five calls per representative. The scores reflected how well the reps performed on a series of items. One of the monitoring staff had to put a rep in Joe's department on a performance management plan because of his consistently low QA scores. Joe listened to some of the recordings and thought that the rep was actually one of the best.

Joe and the representative's team leader went to meet with Lauren, the QA manager. Lauren pulled the rep's file, which showed that he frequently neglected to use the required value-added phrase at the end of each call, despite repeated coaching attempts. "But this representative has gotten more customer compliments than any other rep," said the team leader.

"That's not what we're here to discuss," said Lauren. "Look, you know as well as anyone. We have 2,000 customer service reps on the phone every day. We can't just have them say whatever pops into their head. We need consistent service. This representative refuses to follow the rules. Besides, the decision to place him on discipline is not yours; it's Mary's, and she already approved it." As soon as the representative heard about the disciplinary action, he quit and got a job at another call center across town.

It became apparent to Joe that finding the right balance between policy and providing service to customers was a huge challenge. He had some ideas about how the team leaders could help representatives meet requirements while still being flexible enough to adapt to most situations, but that would require a different way of thinking about each call. He knew the problem — it was obvious from listening to the recordings. Reps were so intent on saying the right phrase that they weren't always listening to what the customer was saying. That had to change.

To help the reps do a better job at finding the right balance between customer needs and internal policies, Joe needed his team leaders to coach their reps to focus more on the customer while still doing the basics, instead of the other way around. Otherwise, reps would continue to recite phrases to avoid getting into trouble, rather than focus on providing great customer service.

"When?" asked one of Joe's team leaders after hearing about his ideas. "We spend four hours a day filling out utilization reports, schedule adherence reports, cross-sale incentive reports, time management spreadsheets, and problem-type coding sheets. Then we're on the phone for another four hours handling escalated calls and filling in for all of the reps who've quit or called in sick. And besides that, we only have 30 minutes each month to meet with our team, and that time is used up explaining that month's changes. Four out of the last five months, even that meeting has been cancelled to handle spikes in call volume."

"Who do I talk to about getting you more time?" asked Joe, determined to fight this battle.

"Workforce Management at HQ," sighed a member of his team. "Good luck with that crowd."

When Joe called the manager of Workforce Management, he was told that the schedule was based on corporate-set targets for productivity, and it could not be changed. Those targets came from the EVP of Operations and were set at the beginning of the year.

Joe had to put his plans aside after that because the last two weeks of the month were consumed with reading and preparing the mountain of reports that he had to finish and forward. He found that he was spending more and more time in his office rather than with his people. And he was getting home later and later. He and his wife began to find reasons to fight, and he ended up missing most of his daughter's waking hours.

A week later, Mary called a meeting with all the service department managers. She announced an exciting new plan that the company developed to improve its service: a new performance management program. All managers would be judged based on the productivity of their employees, the average call handle time of their teams, cross sales, and quality monitoring scores. The company was holding each of them personally accountable for achieving substantial improvements in each metric.

Joe stopped by Mary's office right after the meeting. "Mary, I am really excited about the new program," he said. "But I have a couple concerns." Mary put down her pen and crossed her arms. "Such as?" she asked.

Joe replied, "Well, for starters, we have some real problems with how we do quality monitoring. It's more about checking the boxes and following exact wording than doing what's right for the customer. Plus, I would love to have my team leaders spend more time working on coaching and employee engagement, but Workforce Management won't give them any time to meet with their staff. Even the monthly meetings are almost always cancelled to handle call volume. And how can we reduce handle time if we have to make more offers to every customer after handling their issue? The two are in direct conflict."

Mary looked right at Joe. "Joe, it's your job to figure that out. To tell you the truth, I'm already hearing concerns. QA and Workforce Management have both expressed to me that you are not a team player and are overstepping your bounds. And you never seem to be on the floor with your team."

Joe was aghast. "I thought you hired me for my ideas," he said.

Mary's stare became even cooler. "We hired you to run a group of call center representatives. If you cannot do that the way we do things here, then we have a bigger problem to deal with. You need to get with the program if this is going to work out. Consider this a formal warning."

So, at 3:00 a.m., Joe made his decision. If he continued to fight to do what he thought was right, he would probably lose his job, and his family would be in serious trouble. Or he could keep his head down, pass the buck like his peers did, and try to stay as invisible as possible until he could find another job. He had no choice. He had to look out for his family first and put his pride aside.

He would start by nominating his worst performer for promotion to lead a team in another department. Without that loser weighing him down, the numbers for his group would instantly improve. "I have to look out for Number One," he thought to himself as he finally drifted off to sleep.

Everyone in Joe's company — his supervisor, the QA manager, Workforce Management, and even the EVP of Operations — faced expectations, rules, policies, and bureaucratic barriers that they believed forced them to behave the way they did. Leaders and managers felt compelled to protect themselves, so they created rules that furthered their own goals, regardless of the damage to the company. The managers created rules and policies designed to eliminate exceptions (like a rep not using the "value-added phrase"), made everyone else follow inflexible processes (like those of the QA department), or focused on one goal at the expense of others (like the scheduling team did by eliminating team meetings) all to bring some control to the situation. Everything was set up to keep others from taking away managers' and leaders' ability to check the box they needed to check.

The problem was that some of these rules made it hard for Joe and his team to do what they needed to do. Then, when faced with a situation in which the rules made no sense, the only thing Joe or his team could say is, "There is nothing we can do." As a result, good people left, innovation died, quality of service was the worst in the industry, and trying to bring about positive change was futile and professionally dangerous.

Despite the best intentions, barriers were born. And they were all self-imposed.

Joe's situation is hardly unique. When faced with bureaucratic barriers, leaders often feel powerless to do anything about them. It became so bad in one organization that its vice president of sales said that for all intents and purposes, he was "the vice president of nothing." So what is it about human nature that leads people to build obstacles that clearly get in the way of an organization's ability to succeed? That question demanded an answer.

My colleagues and I at Gallup worked with several companies that had "stalled." No matter what they tried, no matter what they did, they just could not stop a slow downward slide. To determine the root cause of this problem, we conducted extensive background material reviews of policies and procedures and conducted several thousand in-depth interviews with people at different organizational levels, from CEOs to frontline employees in different industries, functions, and job types in both the public and private sectors, across a dozen countries spanning six continents.

The focus of this research was to identify policies, practices, and procedures that hindered success — often without an apparent good reason — and then to trace the origin of the problem. In every case, the problem was a barrier: something put in place internally that was intended to help one group but harmed another. When we examined the data, we found that one root cause for those barriers far overshadowed all others. It existed in every organization that we studied and was generally the driving force behind the most damaging and most severe barriers. It was fear — fear of loss.

What largely drove that fear of loss, we further discovered, was an endemic sense of entitlement. Whether the issue was pay, a bonus, a promotion, decision rights, a big office, headcount, or a budget, people would go to great lengths to protect something they felt they were entitled to — even if doing so was not in the best interest of the organization as a whole. The victims of these protective decisions often knew how harmful these behaviors were, but they were powerless to do anything about them.

Why would intelligent and dedicated people put up barrier after barrier to try to protect their entitlements and agendas, even if it increases the odds of losing everything or clearly harms the organization? The answer, according to Daniel Kahneman, a Princeton psychologist who won the 2002 Nobel Prize in Economics, and his longtime colleague Amos Tversky, is because it is in our nature. We can't help it.

Kahneman and Tversky's Prospect Theory suggests that once someone feels entitled to something, the pain of having to give up that entitlement is much more intense than the pleasure that would come from an incremental gain of the same size. For example, if someone is used to getting a 3% raise every year, then a 2% raise would be demoralizing, depressing, and demotivating, even if the trade-off is better job security for the next 10 years. The pleasure of that security pales in comparison to the pain of giving up what that person believes he deserves now. Even though it is a gain, it feels like a loss. On the other hand, if someone is used to getting a 1% raise, that same 2% would seem like a gift because he would not be "giving up" anything to get it. Yet it's the same 2%. In one case, it's a gain; in one case, it's a loss. The only difference is the person's perception of what he deserves.

What made Kahneman and Tversky's discoveries even more profound lies in the psychology of gains and losses: How people feel is *not* determined by the actual amount of the gain or the loss. That's not what determines its value. Rather, the value of an outcome depends on *what they expected*, or their own personal "reference point." Any outcome lower than what they expected will feel like a loss — even if it's technically a gain.

KAHNEMAN AND TVERSKY'S PROSPECT THEORY

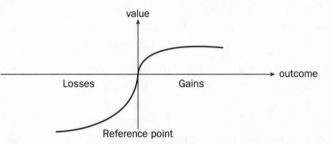

As shown in the graph, anything above a "reference point" or expectation level is considered a gain, while anything below it is considered a loss. The shape of the curve shows that there is much more pain from falling short of a reference point than joy from exceeding it. Adapted from Kahneman, D., & Tversky, A. *Prospect theory: An Analysis of Decision Under Risk,* March 1979.

Expectation is powerful. It doesn't take long for people to feel entitled to what they have and become worried about losing it. The threat of loss isn't just about money. People can fear losing ownership over a particular area, not getting that corner office, losing headcount, or even having to give up a title or perks. Instinct will drive people to fight to keep from losing what they have or what they feel they deserve, or both. That's not necessarily a bad thing. The desire to compete and win, to fight and conquer, is what inspires people to build businesses and is the motivation that makes those companies successful. But fear turned inward can be lethal. When threatened, people's natural inclination is to fight or grab what they can and run — fight or flight.

So in the face of fear of loss, the motivation to sacrifice now for some potential later gain may not be very compelling. As a result, people may feel the need to protect their ability to get a bonus even if it means gaming the system. They might feel the need to protect their budget even if it means unnecessary spending at the end of the year so they won't lose those funds when budgeting time comes around. They might hoard information or add unnecessary policies and rules to keep others at bay and to protect their turf.

In the sales and marketing division of a large global manufacturing company, the finance department assumed so much control over everything that it could bring the entire company to a standstill. No one could spend a penny, even for approved budgets, without going through several layers of approval first. The costs in disengagement, turnover, and lost sales opportunities were massive. But the finance department was secure.

All too often, people face a basic dilemma between what is best for them personally versus what is best for the organization. It's hard to apply cold impersonal logic in the face of such a strong drive to protect and survive, especially if the feelings are at odds with each other. Barriers inevitably spring up when these two dynamics are in conflict. But when they are in perfect alignment, organizations can avoid these types of barriers.

Successfully managing this basic balancing act, the survival instinct of the individual versus the operational needs of the greater good, is a leadership imperative that is all too often overlooked. It is a theme we will see again and again. If these two forces are not managed properly, fear of loss can become a self-fulfilling prophecy.

Chapter Two:

PAROCHIALISM

Fear creates barriers. But barriers don't spring up overnight. They evolve.

As businesses grow, their operating model becomes more complex. In a small company, people often share responsibilities or wear multiple hats, but expansion inevitably requires division of responsibilities or a more narrow focus for specific departments. This means specialized job roles. Organizations need to create a human resources department, maybe along with a separate recruiting and training group. They might form a legal department to manage the exposure that comes from increasing the complexity of the business or to create contracts they now need with a wider range of suppliers and customers. They'll divide up functional responsibilities such as sales versus marketing strategies and tactics.

As organizations establish different functions, they have to hire people to lead each one. So managers are put in charge of different areas and given responsibility for their specific area's success. In effect, people are endowed with departments. That's all well and good — and necessary. It would be wasteful for a company to reengineer itself every time a functional area's purview changed or expanded. But when growth is not handled properly, the seeds of bureaucracy are planted. And it all comes back to fear of loss.

The person in charge of a particular function will, of course, be judged primarily on how well that function performs. As business grows, other departments will inevitably have increasing demands for customization, exceptions, and quicker turnarounds on the more specialized groups. At the same time, all of these departments will begin to compete for resources, budget, IT initiatives, and headcount.

So how do the leaders of these functions survive in the face of all of those demands and not lose control? They create rules, standards, and policies to bring order to the growing chaos. Rules are, in a sense, walls that provide boundaries within which people must operate. Sometimes, though, the walls get so high that those behind them lose sight of the world outside.

When they do, they lose sight of the most important thing: the overall mission or strategy. To them, everything revolves around what's important to the *department* — their ability to complete their part of the process and check off that one box, regardless of whether or not it supports the larger strategic goals. The ultimate outcome, customer-related or financial, may start to become more and more disconnected from everyday work and decision making.

As this phenomenon becomes increasingly severe, those behind the walls will be tempted to view the world not through the eyes of the customer, but strictly through the filter of their part of the process. The focus on process over outcomes becomes the norm. Those within the group start to define success as completing their part of the job, regardless of the impact on others. They start thinking in terms of "my department" not "our company." Their world becomes defined by the piece, rather than the puzzle.

Inevitably, situations will arise for which there's no set policy. What *should* happen is whatever is in the best interest of the company. What often *does* happen is whatever is in the best interest of one particular function. As one employee put it, "We've had a very metrics-driven culture to the point of dysfunction. We've blurred the lines between means to an end and the end. We have many managers who can't connect the dots, and as a result, the colleagues suffer." This is especially noticeable in companies that are under pressure.

For example, when the financial services industry was first hit by the recession, many companies in the industry went to extreme measures to control costs. The supply department of one company faced great pressure to stay within its targets. As a result, the head of the supply department declared a three-month moratorium on new orders. The employees still needed basic materials — things like pens and printer ink — but they weren't allowed to order more. That left branch managers with two options: If they were short on paper, for example, they could go to an office supply store and buy some for about five dollars, but they would not get reimbursed. Or they could make a request from corporate supply and get reprimanded. Neither of these options was very attractive.

Instead, a smart branch manager would call another manager somewhere else in the country and barter: three reams of paper, say, for a case of paper clips. And for several hundred dollars in shipping between branches, the company saved the five dollars that the paper cost at the store. An entire black market over supplies sprung up overnight. Nevertheless, the head of supply was recognized for keeping that department's budget under control.

When this kind of thing happens — functional silos creating protective policies and rules, defining success by focusing on only what happens in their own little world, and losing sight of the ultimate outcome — a company has reached the first level of bureaucracy: Parochialism. Parochialism is the base of the pyramid of bureaucracy. Each level of the pyramid builds on the one before it, creating more and more barriers with each step. This foundational level begins with redefining success based on what is best for one part of an organization — the underlying cause of the harm that parochialism generates for others.

THE PYRAMID OF BUREAUCRACY

Level One:
PAROCHIALISM

With parochialism, the world is strictly contained within the walls of a particular function. Maintaining the standards of that function takes precedence over creating engaged customers and business success. Information is evaluated through a narrow filter, and decisions are made for the benefit of the silo. Those decisions may not match the company's needs; those needs may not even be considered. Business success becomes defined as simply completing the process that the function has created. Reality, customers, and the marketplace become peripheral — if those within the parochial function notice them at all.

Sustaining parochialism isn't easy. It takes a lot of effort. So to deal with incessant interruptions, exceptions, and problems, parochial departments (and often whole companies) make new rules to protect themselves: rules that control actions, rules that restrict the flow of information, rules that limit and define how others will deal with that department, rules about the rules for changing the rules — all to serve the parochial needs of a local "ruler."

Of course, not all rules are bad. Every organization needs policies and procedures to protect itself and to define acceptable behavior. A rule evolves into a barrier only when the amount of good it prevents outweighs the amount of bad it protects against. In other words, rules that *protect the organization more than they prevent success* are beneficial. Rules that *prevent success more than they protect the organization* are the building blocks of parochial fear-based barriers.

Rules tend to enforce parochialism when they are absolute. Think of absolute rules as *gospels*. They never go away. They are never questioned, and there are absolutely no exceptions. Not all gospels are bad, though. For instance, airplane passengers must keep their seat belts fastened during takeoff and landing. That rule ensures everyone's safety.

Other gospels are not as wise. General Motors (GM) used to have a rule that senior executives had to review presentations three times: They'd read the presentation before the meeting, sit through the presentation, and read the minutes of the presentation afterward. This is part of the reason why GM executives routinely read 600-700 pages of documents a day, ranging from divisional performance results to lease agreements, leaving them with little time for selling cars.

Helpful rules promote an organization's ability to serve customers or to achieve a strategic outcome. Parochial rules benefit someone internal, possibly at the expense of the desired outcome. When rules that benefit one parochial group *at the expense of* the success of another group begin to appear, then the rules become a barrier. Unfortunately, violating these parochial rules in the name of doing what's right for customers or the company can end up getting you in very deep and very hot water.

As treacherous as defying the rules can be, it's even more dangerous to try to destroy them. The walls around parochial fortresses are likely to be well-fortified. And attempts at breaching these walls can be akin to political suicide. As Admiral Hyman Rickover said, "If you're going to sin, sin against God, not the bureaucracy. God will forgive you but the bureaucracy won't."

It's important to remember that these rules aren't created out of avarice. The way people process information is based on the context within which they frame the information. Depending on your frame of reference, you can reach different conclusions from the same set of facts. Different groups may have different reference points regarding the necessary level of performance for a particular outcome. It stands to reason, then, that when people feel great ownership over a particular area, their primary focus will be on how events affect their department — often without too much concern about how events will affect the company as a whole.

None of this is a matter of selfishness or greed. It is simply how people are wired. Fortunately, it's also rather formulaic: If you know how someone views and interprets the world, you will understand how parochialism evolves. And you'll know why the parochial feel so strongly that they're doing the right thing. Managers and leaders who are acting in a parochial manner don't think they're doing anything wrong. Often it is the contrary: They strongly believe that they are taking a courageous stand for what is best. They may have even been rewarded for their actions even though those actions are clearly harming the organization.

Behavioral economist George Loewenstein's study on behavioral decision theory and business ethics helps to explain this phenomenon of doing something that is clearly wrong but thinking it is right. He found that "whenever individuals face tradeoffs between what is best for themselves and what is morally correct, their perceptions of moral correctness are likely to be biased in the direction of what is best for themselves." In other words, if your self-interests are in conflict with those of the greater good, it is simply human nature for you to adjust your view of the greater good to match the context of what is best for you.

For example, a manager may have a goal to hit a certain budget, which she believes she can only meet by following a set process. If a situation comes up that requires altering the process, possibly at the expense of that manager meeting her goal, she will have a natural inclination to fight against what she sees as an incursion on her turf. Her reaction is not entirely her fault. If organizations do not aggressively work to prevent situations in which one individual or group succeeds at the expense of others, the leaders of those groups may feel compelled to act in a parochial manner. If an organization is holding leaders accountable to hit certain goals, and others appear to be getting in the way, then it is logical for leaders to feel justified putting up walls and barriers to prevent those interruptions or distractions from having any effect — even if doing so ultimately hurts the broader organization.

Chapter Three:

TERRITORIALISM

In 1993, IBM hired Louis Gerstner, Jr. as CEO. He said that the IBM of the time was a "hermetically sealed" world with turf wars, three separate budgets, a slow management system, facilities scattered all over the world, 70 different ad agencies, and control largely in the hands of a management committee that had a tremendous amount of power but little accountability. Gerstner said that operating this way gave IBM "a foxhole mentality." That mentality is what caused a legendarily innovative company to become very nearly inert.

Many managers can relate to this situation. In every company, fulfilling each department's needs requires resources — and there is only so much to go around. Competition over resources can become intense, particularly during budget season; budgets require tough decisions. There are usually more worthwhile requests than there are resources available, even in the best of times. To many department leaders, decisions become less about what's "equitable" and more about how to get their projects pushed through, no matter what happens to other departments.

The battle for resources intensifies with growth. Every department has a list of initiatives and pet projects, and the more departments, the more voices there are clamoring for funds. The company has a responsibility to allocate resources in a way that best enables it to meet its overall strategic goals. However, the goals of individual departments may become harder to achieve if managers can't get the resources they request. So what does a manager do?

Often, managers feel that they have no choice but to maintain the tightest level of control possible over people and budgets to ensure that no penny is wasted and no assets are lost, especially to other departments. They may pressure frontline workers to meet short-term goals at the expense of meeting their specific departmental goals. By doing so, these managers create even thicker barriers to protect their turf.

These barriers institutionalize the problem of fear. If managers are worried enough, they may feel forced to start controlling resources, projects, and people just to maintain control. They believe this is a solution to a temporary problem, but it rarely is. What starts out as a fear-based reaction can soon become standard operating procedure. Tight control becomes more and more prevalent, and it inevitably affects interdepartmental behavior. The whole scenario creates a low-grade siege mentality.

This condition is the second level of the pyramid of bureaucracy: territorialism.

THE PYRAMID OF BUREAUCRACY

Level Two:
TERRITORIALISM

Level One:
PAROCHIALISM

To be clear about terms, parochialism and territorialism differ in various ways. They are the result of different dynamics, and they have different manifestations: While parochialism is about protection from *outside*, territorialism is about control over what is *inside*, regardless of the impact on frontline staff or other departments. While parochialism and territorialism are not the same thing, they are not mutually exclusive. A parochial manager can also be territorial, and vice versa.

A parochial manager focuses on controlling those outside her sphere of influence to make them see things her way. A territorial manager focuses on controlling those inside his area to maintain a tight grip on resources. A parochial manager will set up unnecessary rules, policies, and procedures to put her local goals ahead of the goals of others or those of the rest of the organization. A territorial manager will seek to maintain absolute control over the people and resources at his disposal.

Taking away freedom. Among the many ways territorial managers exercise control, one of the most common is to limit employees' empowerment by taking away their freedom. Low empowerment, despite high levels of accountability, is a serious barrier that exists to some degree in virtually all organizations. Limited empowerment is especially common with customer-facing employees. No company would say that it wants to hire brainless robots with no free will. And yet all too often, companies script every word and deed of frontline employees, not allowing them to make any decisions whatsoever, while holding them solely responsible for their results.

No matter how well-intentioned scripting is, it almost always backfires. For example, if a representative is unable to solve a customer's problem, if the customer is clearly in a hurry, or if the representative isn't empowered to actually help, uttering a phrase as harmless as "Is there anything else I can help you with?" at the end of a service encounter adds insult to irritation. Even something as innocuous as telling representatives to smile throughout transactions can drive customers into a frenzy. A customer who is angry and upset will be even more infuriated by a rep who just grins while the customer rants about why he is dissatisfied.

It's impossible to script every customer-employee interaction. But companies still try because it's an attempt to control the situation — and the employee. One bank offered call center service seven days a week, 365 days a year, even though the rest of the company was closed on weekends and holidays. One Presidents' Day, a call center representative received a call from a customer who wanted to set up an automatic billing plan. The phone rep would have had to transfer the customer to another department to set up the automatic payment, but it was a holiday, and the other department was closed.

The representative offered the customer three options: The rep could contact the customer at another time that was convenient for him, she could give the customer the direct number to the other department to call the next day, or the customer could call back during regular business hours and any customer service rep could transfer him to the right place. The customer chose the second option, seemed satisfied, and the call ended.

That call was randomly selected by quality assurance for monitoring, and it earned a failing grade, causing the rep to lose her bonus for the month. Why? Because the rule said that if a call needed to be transferred, then the rep must attempt the transfer. There was no provision for if the department was closed. Ultimately, controlling what the representative said and did was more important than allowing her to serve her customer properly — and the rep still believes she lost her bonus for choosing to do the right thing.

Taking away extra time. Every job requires a certain amount of time to perform. Territorialism systematically fills every minute with bare-minimum tasks, leaving no time for outstanding performance and certainly none for personal empowerment. The accompanying scarcity of resources forces employees to work at maximum capacity to meet their local goals, with no room or time for anything else. If an employee does not have the time to step outside the process or go the extra mile for a customer or associate, the territorial rule remains intact because the employee simply won't have time to break it.

In one hospital, a clinical staff member told us through tears of frustration that in the past, she was able to take the time to comfort patients and try to make them feel at ease. But as the hospital grew, it pressured staff to boost patient throughput. That employee no longer had time to comfort patients and instead felt like she had to tell them to "lie down, shut up, sit still, and get out." To boost that department's numbers, time pressure stripped away her empowerment.

Eliminating opportunities to gain knowledge or skills. Employees have to try new things and acquire skills to move into new areas of responsibility. In times of scarcity, training is often the first thing to go, even though that training may help prepare employees for transfers, advancement, or new ways of doing things. Lack of a particular competency will render them powerless, and as a result, controlled. Leaders seldom cut or limit training opportunities out of malice, but the end result is the same. It guarantees that employees will stay inside the territorial walls built by those in control.

Restricting information flow. Employees who don't know what's going on are extremely dependent on their manager. That gives managers more power than they are entitled to and creates a bottleneck of information, which is another form of control. If managers keep employees in the dark — about issues as major as strategy or as minor as office supply entitlements — they limit employee participation and effectiveness. Moreover, lack of knowledge makes it virtually impossible for employees to suggest ideas or to get approval for exceptions. In one manufacturing company, the innovation program was nicknamed the "Black Hole." Once employees made a suggestion, they never heard anything about it again. One hospital gave e-mail access to only one-third of its employees, and yet it communicated most major initiatives and solicitations for input, of course, via e-mail.

Withholding support. Perhaps the most insidious way for a territorial manager to limit empowerment is to implicitly or explicitly express that employees are empowered at their own risk and that they will not be supported if things go south. One college chairperson told his assistant that she should never learn to do anything exceptionally well because it would make the department's other assistants feel inferior, and he didn't want to have to hear their complaints. A newly promoted manager in a healthcare manufacturing company was told by one of his peers, "You should never hire anyone who might seem to be smarter than you. You always want someone to blame if things go wrong, so make sure your hires don't get promoted above you."

This type of control keeps employees from using their talents, stifles innovation, and prevents leaders from being either outshined or embarrassed. And because withholding support is interpersonal and subjective, territorial managers can easily refute that they've done it.

But territorialism isn't just about controlling people. *Everything* counts to a territorial manager. An automobile manufacturer's U.S. operations moved its knowledge management group into the customer relations organization, which included a call center for customers and dealers. The knowledge management group was previously located in the headquarters building, where it helped provide information for strategic decisions. The call center group needed information, such as the customer database, that the knowledge group tightly controlled. In the ensuing battle over control of the customer database, relations between the two groups quickly deteriorated. The problem became so severe that the new leadership of customer relations created an entirely new alignment strategy with new roles and responsibilities. Her stated goal was to "tear down the Berlin Wall that we have built between the two groups."

That was a courageous — and smart — decision. But even companies that make conscious efforts to keep walls from forming will see territorialism rear its head during budget season. Toward the close of the fiscal year, companies often have leftover money: unspent budget dollars, abandoned projects, or initiatives that have come in under projected costs. Rather than giving up those resources, territorial departments may go on a "shopping spree" to use up budgets before the end of the fiscal year because next year's budget allocation depends on this year's spending. So territorial managers may request to be billed far in advance or create new projects not in the plan — even though another group may have desperately needed that money to reach the goals they now will miss.

This practice sounds vaguely corrupt, but in most cases, it's actually a fairly typical human response to the perception of ownership. Many of these seemingly selfish decisions can be explained by what's called the endowment effect: Once someone believes he either owns or is entitled to something, he places higher value on it.

In a 1990 endowment effect study conducted by Daniel Kahneman, Jack L. Knetsch, and Richard H. Thaler, in one group (the "buyers"), subjects were shown a coffee mug and asked what they would pay for it. In the second group (the "sellers"), subjects were given the same mug and asked what price they would sell it for. The median price that the buyers, or the "non-endowed," would pay was $2.25. The median price at which the sellers, or the "endowed" group, would sell was $5.78. It was the same mug. The only difference was that one group owned the mug; the other group did not.

Nearly everyone who has put up a house for sale has experienced the endowment effect. And in a typical market, buyers will disabuse sellers of their idea that the house is worth what the endowment effect suggests it is. But there aren't many people who are willing to tell territorial managers that their notions of entitlement are inflated. Once leaders or managers believe they own something, they may go to great lengths to protect it and their ownership of it. They will assign a greater value to that resource, no matter what it is, than will others in the organization — and they will often fight to protect it.

"We have a terrible printer," sighed one study group participant. "Most of my workplace stress is related to that printer. But when our manager told us that we might have to give up our printer and share with the other department on our floor, we were all furious. Even though their printer is better, it's across the hall, and the other department only has five people in it. We hate our printer, but we refused to give it up."

The longer people feel ownership over something, the more powerful the endowment effect becomes. In a 1998 article on the endowment effect, Michal Strahilevitz and George Loewenstein explained that not only do people place a higher value on something they own but that "object valuation is affected by both past and present ownership status — that is, by the history of ownership." Length of ownership, previous ownership, and the amount of time since losing ownership all influence perceptions of value.

When Lou Gerstner took over at IBM, the endowment effect wasn't just a psychological quirk — it was standard operating procedure for all the company's territorial managers. Having gone through all the "foxholes" at

IBM — foxholes dug and furiously defended by territorial leaders — Gerstner's first order of business was eradicating territorialism. During his first month, he disbanded the management committee, which originated and functioned as the engine of territorialism at IBM. He replaced this committee with the Corporate Executive Committee and at the same time, created the Worldwide Management Council. The Worldwide Management Council's primary purpose was, according to Gerstner, to "get the executive team working together as a group with common goals — and not to act as some United Nations of sovereign countries. These meetings represented a chance for our top executives to grab one another and say, 'I've got a great idea, but I need your help.'"

By the time Gerstner retired from IBM in 2002, he had rescued the company from the brink of disaster, created several new lines of business, and put Big Blue back in the forefront of business computers. Many factors and variables drove IBM's remarkable turnaround, but the thing Gerstner said he was proudest of was that his successor and the heads of all the major business units were longtime IBM employees. He had taught his people how to fill in their own foxholes, tear down the barriers, and vaporize fear. If IBM can break through barriers, so can other companies.

Chapter Four:
EMPIRE BUILDING

Territorial managers and leaders can control their fiefdoms unchecked as long as they don't have to deal with other departments. But when they do, fear of loss of their ability to maintain control can drive them to spread their sphere of power over others. And that's when fear reaches its apex in an organization: when individual departments start building empires. Empire building is the pinnacle and most extreme level of the pyramid of bureaucracy, often existing as an attempt to defend against the parochialism and territorialism of others.

THE PYRAMID OF BUREAUCRACY

Level Three:
EMPIRE BUILDING

Level Two:
TERRITORIALISM

Level One:
PAROCHIALISM

Empire building occurs when one group attempts to regain or enhance its self-sufficiency by encroachment or by expanding its span of control even when that is not in the best interest of the organization. There are several signs that empire building has begun: Departments compete for IT initiatives. Recruiting may become backlogged. Leaders either directly or indirectly control other independent groups by "speaking for them"; by claiming the right to prioritize time or resources for different departments; or in empire building's most severe form, by creating duplicate functions of their own.

Empire building cannot exist without parochialism and territorialism. The preconditions for empire building are endemic fear, different views of success, tight control over resources, and lack of shared accountabilities — the bricks and mortar of parochialism and territorialism. When faced with parochial and territorial colleagues and the barriers they build, managers might feel that they have no other choice *but* to build empires.

But empire building is not the same as parochialism and territorialism. Parochial managers do not necessarily want to take control over other departments. Instead, they build walls against others' empire building attempts to keep outsiders from interfering with their own local focus and viewpoint. Territorialism is about keeping things just the way they are; empire building is about changing the balance of power. While territorialism seeks to impose limits over what people can do inside the silo, empire building seeks to change the focus of what those in *other* departments do. Territorialism is about defending the current span of control, but empire building is about expanding it.

Empire building can take many forms, but it's fundamentally about acquisition and expansion. Empire builders are driven to take over headcount, information, budgets, decision rights, or other resources. When they do, it creates inefficiency, conflict, and disengagement — and it wastes resources. Instead of worrying about a competitor taking over a segment of the market, empire builders worry about asserting control within their own companies. Time and money end up being directed at internal turf wars rather than at external competition. Empire building is not the valid consolidation of oversight, but rather the deliberate attempt to improve one group's self-sufficiency at the expense of another group's success. The costs to an organization can be enormous.

For example, a multibillion-dollar company centralized several support functions under its head of human resources. As a result, that executive became chief administrative officer over human resources, accounts payable, legal, real estate, and several other departments. Although the IT needs of the businesses were specialized in research and development, she insisted that IT should also be under her charge and successfully fought to add IT to her growing empire. The outcome was inefficiency, wasted resources, disengagement, and lack of focus, all of which resulted in unnecessary costs for the organization.

One financial services company decided to expand its suite of products in an effort to grow customer relationships and revenue. The company created a new products group in the customer service organization to lead the charge and to act as a liaison between marketing, sales, and service in developing and launching new add-on products and services. In creating these services and programs, the company had to expend significant resources to reprogram the customer databases, the interactive voice response (IVR) system, and the website. If those changes were not implemented, it would be difficult for the new products group to hit its objectives. Unfortunately, there was a long list of IT initiatives scheduled to be completed first.

In the face of this loss of self-sufficiency, the new products group decided to hire its own programmers, testing staff, and computer support personnel, even though others in the customer service group were simultaneously changing the same programs. This redundancy led to immense waste: duplicate headcount, conflicting IT priorities, systems problems, and the need for management to constantly referee. It was only after a costly restructuring — in which nearly 100 manager and supervisory positions were eliminated — that the organization addressed the problem. Duplicate functions require duplicate headcount and budgets. In a few isolated cases, this may be justified, but in most cases, it's simply wasteful and inefficient.

The financial costs are just the beginning. When two separate groups control the same function, inevitably they will want to go in different and sometimes conflicting directions. Groups might hide information or plans from another group just because they know the other group would object, possibly resulting in bad feelings or broken internal partnerships. This forces management to step in to arbitrate, wasting even more time and resources.

The desire to build empires does not necessarily stem from greed. It stems from the fear that unless a group seizes control from others, the project or the group will fail in some way. Often, organizations will permit or overlook an empire builder's encroachment because he presents his attempt at conquest as a faster way to meet an objective. In other cases, the empire builder is more subtle, taking over inch by inch. By the time anyone notices, the change has already occurred.

At that point, leadership may decide that it's easier just to let the groups fight it out, regardless of the long-term consequences or barriers that may result. But make no mistake, if empire building meets the needs of one group at the expense of another, it will harm the organization.

Lenovo, the Chinese computer manufacturing company, presents an interesting example of empire building. Liu Chuanzhi created Lenovo in a two-room Beijing guardhouse in 1984. It quickly grew into a behemoth, capturing about a third of the Chinese market. Chuanzhi outmaneuvered every trap while managing Lenovo, from government controls to management problems to economic dangers. By 2005, Lenovo completed its acquisition of IBM's Personal Computing Division along with its executive team, making it a global IT competitor. Shortly after, Chuanzhi stepped down and let the newly merged management team take over.

That's when the trouble started. There were not only cultural clashes, but philosophical divisions and lack of competency in several areas. By 2008, Lenovo's leaders were so focused on their empires that they didn't have attention to spare for consumers and small businesses that were fed up with Lenovo's products. Fortunately, Chuanzhi stepped back in. "Lenovo was like somebody standing on the edge of a cliff," he said. "Lenovo is all of my life. When it looked like my life was threatened, I had to come out to defend it." Chuanzhi sat by while a few executive contracts expired, let a few other leaders go, swiftly dismantled the empires by narrowing down the executive committee, and reinstituted the management practices that made Lenovo what it had been before he left. By 2010, Lenovo had a cohesive team with a long list of new products to launch. PC shipments were more than twice the industry average, and Lenovo was back on track.

Chapter Five:
THE COST OF FEAR

As noted earlier, two of the hallmarks of fear-based bureaucracies are excessive limits on empowerment and holding people accountable for local goals at the expense of larger success. When a manager behaves in a territorial manner — controlling staff through low empowerment or misguided accountability — employees have trouble assisting with, or even seeing, what's happening in the organization as a whole.

To discover how prevalent territorial behavior is in American workplaces, Gallup conducted a nationally representative study of 2,634 U.S. working adults in January 2007. Gallup asked respondents in the study about various aspects of empowerment and accountability in their workplace as an indication of how much they were controlled versus how they were judged. While we can't exactly ask managers if they are being territorial, we *can* ask employees about their current levels of empowerment and accountability. For example, respondents were asked to rate the degree to which they agreed or disagreed with each of the following statements (using a 5-point scale with 5 being "strongly agree").

Aspects of empowerment:

- I have the freedom I need to make necessary decisions.

- I have time to complete all of my assigned tasks with a high level of quality.

- I have the training and development I need to do my work right.

- I have the materials and equipment I need to do my work right.

- My manager or supervisor always supports and encourages my success.

- At work, my opinions seem to count.

Aspects of accountability:

- My success is judged based on clear, objective metrics that I can impact directly.

- In the past six months, I have been given feedback on my performance.

- There are clear and objective rewards for meeting or exceeding my goals.

- There are clear and objective penalties for not meeting my goals.

- My manager holds me highly accountable for achieving results.

- I always trust my company to be fair to all employees.

From the resulting data set, we categorized workers into four groups based on their levels of empowerment and accountability: Top Performers, Loose Cannons, Broken Spirits, and Prisoners.

Top Performers are not necessarily Top Performers in their job, but in theory, it is *possible* for them to become Top Performers. They have high average levels of agreement with the empowerment and accountability statements (a mean score of 4.0 or greater on both dimensions). These are the kinds of employees who approach a customer problem by saying, "I am here to help," who are *able* to help, and who expect their manager to know about it and approve. Top Performers represent about one-fourth of the U.S. working population.

Loose Cannons are highly empowered — too much so. They have great power but very little responsibility. Loose Cannons reported that they are not held strictly accountable for their actions: They have no objective metrics, don't receive feedback on their performance, and/or face no consequences for their actions. Rather, they are totally free to do as they please without metrics and without being held in check by their managers. Loose Cannons may respond to valid objections by saying, "Do it anyway because I said so." Loose Cannons make up 21% of the U.S. working population.

Broken Spirits are held highly accountable but have little, if any, empowerment. Members of this group have certain firm metrics and face consequences for falling short of performance targets. However, they are completely unable to make decisions or adapt to new situations. Broken Spirits have little leeway to solve customer problems and may instead be reduced to quoting a policy, reading a script, pleading that it's not part of their job, or just giving up and handing the problem off to a manager, saying, "Our policy prevents me from helping you" or just reading the same scripted phrase over and over again. Broken Spirits represent the smallest proportion, accounting for 5% of the U.S. working population.

Prisoners lack any empowerment and live in a world of shifting rules and subjective accountability. They are caught in a tide, can barely keep their heads above water, and are powerless to do anything about it. Prisoners may simply shrug their shoulders and say, "I'm sorry, but there is nothing I can do" when faced with a customer problem. Prisoners are the ones most likely to be found in a parochial or territorial environment. Shockingly, *one out of every two* American workers is a Prisoner.

Clearly, many workers are victims of bureaucratic, fear-based barriers. While that's bad for these individuals, it is also bad for businesses. To see how much damage these fear-based barriers were doing, the next step was to determine the cost implications of employing Prisoners versus employing Top Performers.

Because this study included a random sample of American workers employed at different organizations, it would be impossible to derive a consistent direct measure of individual business success. Every company measures success differently, as do different departments within companies. However, it is possible to determine the cost of employing Prisoners indirectly using Gallup's Q^{12} employee engagement measure, which has reliably shown strong relationships to business performance across different organizations, industries, levels, job types, countries, and sectors for decades. The Q^{12} assessment was derived by identifying, from a database of thousands of questions and hundreds of thousands of employee responses, items that consistently showed a stable statistical relationship to business outcomes such as productivity, turnover, safety, profitability, and other critical success factors.

Other items on the survey allowed for rough estimates of the business impact of empowerment and accountability. Gallup maintains a vast database of all the Q^{12} responses it collects, so we can calculate percentile rankings to identify different levels of overall performance. For example, if a workgroup's engagement levels are similar to the average workgroup's engagement levels, then its engagement scores would be near the 50th percentile. The 75th percentile is considered to be best in class, and the 90th percentile is considered to be world-class.

Organizations that have a highly engaged workforce consistently outperform organizations with engagement levels that are measurably lower. When engagement is lower, productivity, profit, employee retention, safety, and earnings per share tend to also be lower.

So what does all that imply for business performance? The average engagement level for Top Performers is at the 87th percentile, making that group among the most engaged employees Gallup has studied. They are also, it follows, the most productive. The average level of engagement for Prisoners is at the 8th percentile, making them among the least engaged and least productive employees. Obviously, limiting empowerment and keeping accountability murky may help managers with their own territorial goals, but given the massive difference in engagement between Top Performers and Prisoners, the costs to the larger organization can be exorbitant. Alarmingly, leaders do not always see those losses, nor the pervasive lack of trust that comes with low engagement.

Top Performers believe in their managers: Nearly three-quarters (72%) of Top Performers strongly agreed that their manager was someone they trusted. One-eighth (13%) of Prisoners felt the same way. Conversely, only 1% of Top Performers strongly disagreed that their manager was someone they trusted, compared to 25% of Prisoners who strongly disagreed. In addition to being more mistrustful, workgroups with Prisoners are less innovative: Top Performers are more than six times more likely than Prisoners to say that their manager is open to new ideas and suggestions (71% versus 11%).

Ultimately, parochialism, territorialism, and empire building make a company less successful, less able to innovate, and more prone to high levels of internal distrust. While the barriers that Prisoners and Broken Spirits face may seem insurmountable, it is important to keep in mind that others did not impose these internal barriers. Because people inside companies build barriers, they can be the ones to destroy them, clearing the way for success. To effectively combat fear-based bureaucratic barriers, a company must be ready and willing to attack the problem on all fronts.

Chapter Six:
OVERCOMING PAROCHIALISM

The first level of bureaucracy, parochialism, arises when division of responsibilities strays into creation of entitlements. These entitlements cause those within a parochial silo to see the world only through their own policies, procedures, and rules. For example, Joe, the customer service manager from Chapter One, faced a situation in which the QA department cared only about scripts, the Workforce Management department cared only about schedules, and representatives were caught in the middle.

There are two steps to addressing parochialism: treating the symptoms and curing the disease. The symptoms of parochialism are rules that prevent more than they protect, making life easier for those within the silo at the expense of the broader organization's success. In 2005, on ABCNews.com, Bob Rosner asked viewers to submit examples of ridiculous rules their companies enforce. Some paraphrased examples include:

- In one company, employees were required to agree in writing that they would keep working in the dark if the power went out. This was in a building with no windows and dangerous gases.

- One business denied rental car expenses if the receipt showed that the renter used the car for fewer than 50 miles. So employees would just drive around the airport until they hit the 50-mile mark.

- One company with remote workers required them to call their managers (on the phone) to report phone outages.

These rules are obviously absurd, but they originated from what someone thought was a genuine business need.

Of course, no organization can exist without rules. Sometimes, rules protect not just the company, but also the company's customers. Organizations in highly regulated industries have rules that enforce how business is conducted to ensure compliance with legal requirements. A rule may be in place to help ensure good customer service or a healthy and more productive workplace or to improve the financial success of the organization. Other rules help to avoid liability or risk. Some help prevent catastrophic failures like a fire, factory shutdown, or plane crash.

Unfortunately, sometimes rules don't have anything to do with customer engagement, a better workplace, limiting risk or liability, or avoiding catastrophes — they exist to make life easier for a small part of the organization without any regard for other more important factors. These rules ensure compliance with the policies of a particular department. And those in that department often fiercely guard and protect their rules.

But who is guarding the guards? Why aren't the rules ever audited — not the rules that are mandated by law, but the rules that are mandated internally by a particular silo, the ones that institutionalize parochialism? Conducting an audit of these rules is a critical part of addressing the symptoms of parochialism.

Obviously, auditing every rule and policy in an organization is impractical. So to identify the rules that you need to audit, start by asking which rules sometimes get in the way and are not mandated by law. Different people from different parts of the organization will have different views about whether a rule is good or bad. Those who benefit from the rule will like it. But those who have to live with its negative repercussions may have several examples of how the rule hurts the overall success of the organization more than it protects it against loss or liability.

One call center had a rule that representatives could not put customers on hold unless it was absolutely necessary. Each representative was held accountable for minimizing the percentage of on-hold calls. But no additional training was scheduled, and representatives had few opportunities to meet with their coaches. If they did not know how to handle a particular issue and couldn't put a customer on hold, they were stuck. So the representatives came up with a clever solution. Instead of putting customers on hold, they just hit the mute button. The on-hold levels dropped dramatically. But in surveys, the percentage of customers saying they were being put on hold actually went up.

Once the organization has identified the debatable rules, the audit can begin. It's best for an outside party to conduct the rules audit to avoid the traps of parochialism and territorialism, as well as to maintain confidentiality and openness of responses.

A rules audit follows six sequential steps:

1. Identify the need that the rule is supposed to fulfill, and evaluate the validity of that need.

2. Assess ownership of the rule.

3. Determine how effective the rule is in meeting its intended need.

4. Find unintended consequences of the rule.

5. Establish the type of rule it is and the type it should be.

6. Adjust and communicate.

Identify the need. Every rule should have a clear, established, and valid need that it fulfills. No exceptions. Once you have identified the intended need, evaluate it in the same context as you would evaluate a rule: Does fulfilling the need help provide better service to customers, create a better workplace, improve financial success, avoid risk or liability, or prevent catastrophe? If the answer is no, then the rule should be eliminated. There may be resistance, particularly from those who benefit from the rule. If the answer is yes, the need is valid. Move on to the next step.

Assess ownership. Assessing rule ownership should be easy, and in many cases, it is. Accounting owns accounting rules, customer service owns customer service rules, and so on. But for a surprisingly large number of rules we studied, nobody really owned them. The rules just grew organically. When no one owns a rule, no one is accountable for deciding whether it's good or bad.

Every fall, a national logistics organization had to update its database to identify the distributors that it was not renewing for the coming year. This process protected the company against having unauthorized distributors listed as active, which was a valid need because doing so avoided risk or liability. For several weeks during this update, the entire department's administrative staff would clear their calendars of all other work so they could change the status of every one of the thousands of distributors to "inactive." Then the administrative staff went through several screens for every active distributor to change "no" (inactive) to "yes" (active). Out of the thousands of distributors in the system, usually only a few dozen were not renewed.

For years, the administrative staff had asked why the default could not be "yes," which would enable them to update only the few dozen that were being cut instead of the thousands that weren't. According to their department head, the default option was "no" because the division president wanted it that way. When the division president was asked why the default was set to "no," he said it was because the department head wanted it that way. The reality was that neither one cared as long as the database was updated accurately. So the division president made the call and asked the department head to change the default response to "yes." The process went from taking several weeks to several hours, saving the company a substantial amount of money in lost productivity.

If a rule or policy has no clear owner, the organization needs to assign one. Finding an owner should not be difficult. If no one wants to take responsibility for a rule and it does not represent a legal requirement, it could likely be eliminated if there's a better way to meet its intended need. When you have identified or assigned an owner for the rule, move on to step three.

Determine effectiveness. Just because an organization has identified a need and created a rule does not guarantee that the rule fulfills the need. Some needs are complex. It's human nature to try to find a simple, "elegant" solution. Sometimes that works; often it doesn't. There is a fine line between elegant and oversimplified. The most pervasive example of oversimplifying is legislating behavior. Rather than create guidelines and focus on outcomes, it is easier to mandate certain behaviors, even if those behaviors are not entirely justified in every situation.

A national home entertainment chain discovered that its customers tended to be more loyal if they felt that employees were genuinely happy to see them. So the CEO created an edict: Within the first few seconds of a customer walking in the door, an employee must greet the customer. From then on, whenever a customer entered the store, half a dozen teenage workers ran up to him, blurted out a greeting, and then ran back to what they had been doing. As a result, customers became *more* likely to feel that the store's employees didn't care about them. If anything, the rule made customers feel like employees were irritated by the interruption. So the CEO sent out a second memo, mandating that employees would *sincerely* greet every customer who comes into the store. You can imagine how that worked out.

The owner of the rule is not the only one who should answer the question of how effective a rule is at meeting a particular need; those the rule supposedly protects should as well. For example, does a particular set of behaviors make customers spend more? If not, adhering to a rule that enforces those behaviors might please supervisors and quality monitoring staff, but the rule is not meeting its intended purpose.

Most organizations already have the metrics to ascertain whether a rule is doing any good; such metrics are part and parcel of strategic plans that clearly outline goals and criteria for success. If success — as defined by measurable goals that contribute to the company's mission — has not been defined, all kinds of barriers are likely to spring up. Alignment cannot happen without a unified purpose.

The problem is that rules aren't measured often. So *find out* if a rule makes customers spend more or not. Find out if employee engagement increases when employees follow the rule. Find out if you have reduced or avoided lawsuits, safety incidents, shutdowns, line interruptions, or other failures or risks since you enacted the rule.

Companies shouldn't have to guess what makes them successful. If the rule doesn't demonstrate that it improves performance, then the rule needs to be scrapped in favor of a different one to meet the intended need. Even if the rule does prove to be effective, the next step of the audit is still necessary: finding unintended consequences of the rule — namely, barriers that affect others' ability to succeed.

Find unintended consequences. Parochialism controls how those inside a department interact with those on the outside. The needs of outsiders are of secondary concern, if of any concern at all, to the insiders. Specifically, those within the parochial walls lose sight of the outside world and as a result, they begin to define success locally rather than organizationally. In the most extreme cases, insiders don't even acknowledge outsiders' needs. It's not that the insiders don't know or understand organizational needs. They're just not connected to the day-to-day functions of that department. If these broader needs are not connected to local needs, they are not considered. If they are not considered, then unintended consequences are likely.

Whether the unintended consequences affect those in the department that created the rules or their internal clients, those consequences can reach far downstream.

In an effort to stem abuse and unnecessary expense, one company instituted a rule for travel reimbursement. It would reimburse dinner expenses only for employees who had to stay somewhere overnight. If employees could get home and did not need to stay in a hotel, then they couldn't expense dinner costs for that evening. In many cases, employees *could* get home the same evening, but it might be very late. The company policy implied that they should go as many as 12 hours without food, if they had lunch at noon and got home at midnight. So employees started to stay at hotels — not because they could not have gotten home, but because they were famished. Instead of just paying the $10 for a quick meal on the road, the company paid for a much more expensive dinner at a restaurant *and* $200 for a hotel. Wisely, the company changed its policy and found that the sales force was happier, hotel costs were reduced, and nobody went without dinner.

To determine if a rule has unintended consequences, auditors need input from a wide range of employees, inside and outside the department that owns the rule, as well as from internal and external customers. If, after a thorough evaluation, there are clearly no major harmful unintended consequences because of the rule, then it is probably fine. If the rule does cause harm downstream, the next step is to establish the type of rule it is and the type it should be moving forward.

Establish rule type. As described in Chapter Two, rules that make up the bricks and mortar of parochialism are usually *gospels*, or rules that must always be followed without exception. But there are other types of rules.

Some rules are *guidelines*. Guidelines apply only under certain conditions — for example, waiving late payment fees only for customers who have had no other delinquent payments in the prior 18 months. Some rules that are gospels should be guidelines. Saying "Is there anything else I can help you with?" at the end of a call is appropriate only if the representative was able to solve the customer's problem in the first place. If this rule is a gospel in your organization and representatives say that line even when they can't help a customer, the customer is likely to get angry and frustrated. If a gospel forces behaviors that are inappropriate for some situations, then changing it to a guideline can effectively prevent any unintended consequences that the rule creates.

Some rules do not dictate specific behaviors. Rather, they establish a boundary that should not and cannot be crossed. These are *ground rules*. As long as employees or customers do not cross a particular line, they can do whatever they think is best. For example, drivers can drive as fast as they want on the freeway, as long as they go faster than 40 miles per hour and slower than 65. The minimum and maximum speed limits represent ground rules.

Ground rules are particularly effective in the customer service arena. Different customers have different needs at different times. Attempts to legislate behavior inevitably fail because it is impossible to predetermine the ideal actions for absolutely every possible customer-employee interaction — though many companies try. Instead, if companies determine ground rules and employees focus on outcomes rather than processes, they encourage individualized service experiences, and for the most part, companies can avoid rules that cause inappropriate behavior.

The most elusive rules are *ghosts.* Ghosts are rules that are not really rules. For example, some believe that saying "bless you" or "God bless you" after a sneeze was originally intended to protect the sneezer from evil spirits or the bubonic plague. Many believe this phrase originated with Pope Gregory VII who suggested saying it to protect a person who sneezed because sneezing at that time was an early symptom of the plague. Others once believed that sneezing temporarily forces a person's soul from his or her body. When this happened, saying "bless you" would prevent evil spirits or Satan from taking control of the soul. Many people still use this phrase when somebody sneezes. The need that led to the rule became obsolete, but the rule — or in this instance, the practice — survived.

Most ghosts evolve the same way. They start off as a practice to cope with a specific situation. But over time, those situations change or simply cease to exist. And yet the rule survives because old habits can be hard to break.

In one sales organization, the reps occasionally needed or wanted to transfer inventory between two customers. Often, those customers were in the same territory.

Sometimes the customers were right across the street from one another. However, to transfer the product, a sales rep couldn't simply carry it from one customer to the other. The rule was that the product had to be packed up and shipped back to the West Coast distribution center, put back on a truck, and then shipped to the next customer. The shipping costs were huge, and the process delayed sales. Everyone lost. The reason for this practice was that the original accounting system wasn't designed to deal with that kind of transaction. But with a few programming changes to the current system, the company was able to easily accommodate local transactions, eliminating the extra cost and loss in sales.

Adjust and communicate. Leaders must clearly communicate changes and adjustments to rule types, owners, needs, and other pertinent information to the entire organization. Some rules may survive the rules audit intact. For these rules, leaders simply need to communicate confirmation and support of the rules to preserve their original intent. Some rules may need slight adjustments. Others may mask deeper issues that the organization needs to resolve. Whatever adjustments the company needs to make, leaders need to clearly communicate all changes so that everyone knows about them.

To resolve opposition to changes, it is critical for managers and leaders to hear any objections to the changes and deal with them privately and fairly. But once that's done, it's done. When communicating changes, all leaders and managers should present a common, united front and describe them positively. They should not tolerate dissent and subversion after the "fair hearing" about the changes.

Overcoming parochialism can have dramatic results in your organization. While at first glance, some rules seem to be iron-clad battlements protecting a parochial silo, a disciplined process such as a rules audit can dismantle the walls of that silo, brick by brick. This may hurt some feelings inside the castle, but there will be much rejoicing on the outside. And once the walls are torn down, you will have treated some of the most painful symptoms of parochialism. The next step is to cure the disease.

If those inside the silo are allowed to operate without being held accountable for what happens to others in the organization, then they have no compelling reason to care if they are creating barriers. Penn Station in New York City is the biggest railway station in America. Amtrak owns the station and leases it to the Long Island Rail Road and New Jersey Transit. Each entity has control over its own concourses. The reason it's so difficult to find where you're going in Penn Station is because none of those organizations has any incentive to coordinate signage. One wayfaring designer who worked with Amtrak asked why Penn Station doesn't have a unified sign system, and he was told it's because the three tenants of the building don't talk to each other.

Amtrak and its tenants aren't intentionally confusing 200 million annual customers. Each company is just displaying parochialism, though probably inadvertently, inside Penn Station. As a result, these companies have a negative impact on those 200 million customers. But when functional units have some accountability for the consequences of their actions, they will be less likely to create parochial barriers.

It's important to keep in mind, however, that an *entire* organization can act in a parochial manner and create barriers not just for its employees, but also for its customers. As much as possible, goals should be measurable, attainable, and focused on outcomes, including the ultimate impact on the brand. Organizations should not eliminate local goals. They should align local goals with a broader stake in the organization. It is really just that simple.

Certainly, coming up with the right metrics, standards, mix of local and shared goals, and other related issues requires careful thought. It may require a complete reset of how an organization implements performance management. *Simple* does not necessarily mean *easy*. An organization may never completely overcome all parochialism, but when the overall mission becomes perfectly aligned with local priorities and common sense prevails over local processes, the battle is largely won.

It all comes back to the idea of reference points from Chapter One. Reference points are essential to curing the disease of parochialism. Aligning local reference points with those of the entire organization and its customers makes it much harder to build parochial walls.

But companies still have to be careful that scarcity of resources is not sustaining the second level of bureaucracy: territorialism. If territorialism still exists, competition over those resources can create parochialism all over again, as departments become less and less willing to share. The good news is that companies can remove territorialism as well.

Chapter Seven:
OVERCOMING TERRITORIALISM

Territorialism is about maintaining control over people and resources inside a silo. So overcoming territorialism involves addressing what the people within that silo are — or more importantly are not — empowered to do and how they are held accountable.

Chapter Three introduced how territorial managers use control to limit employees' empowerment, including:

- taking away freedom to make decisions

- taking away time

- eliminating training opportunities

- restricting access to information or resources
- limiting employee participation and innovation
- withholding managerial support

The first step to creating appropriate levels of empowerment is to determine the factors that are limiting it. To find out, companies can conduct an employee survey in which workers indicate how much they agree or disagree with empowerment issues like those in Chapter Five. Once organizations establish which aspects of empowerment are a problem, they can take appropriate corrective action.

Freedom to make decisions. If employees lack the freedom to make decisions, it's probably because of their workgroup's territorial manager. In some cases, a regulatory environment dictates limits on decision-making freedom, but that type of restriction has nothing to do with territorialism. The lack of freedom that comes with territorialism is rooted in employees' fear of the terrible consequences that will result if they overstep their bounds.

When managers don't allow their staff to make any decisions whatsoever, they exhibit a lack of trust. What's more, these managers either forget or don't realize that trust is reciprocal. It's based on mutual respect, a focus on a common goal, and an established set of guiding principles. No manager would say she wants to hire people who can't think for themselves. But territorial environments may lead some managers to force their employees to act that way. As a result of this lack of freedom and trust, their employees' talent is untapped. These situations can often create simmering resentment.

Determining the appropriate level of employees' decision-making freedom comes down to establishing a shared, unifying, mission-oriented company goal and a reasonable set of ground rules. That goal should then become the ultimate barometer of good and bad decisions. The mission orientation is not focused on any single department, but on what the company *at large* aspires to become to its employees, customers, and shareholders. As long as workers are acting within the established guidelines and ground rules, they should be able to determine the best course of action to take.

Southwest Airlines wants to make flying fun and to enable more people to fly. The Ritz-Carlton has aligned its entire organization with creating memorable and luxurious experiences for its guests. Those goals are not focused on a specific department but on a desired organizational outcome. Yet they have everything to do with how leaders and employees in specific departments should act — and how they should make decisions.

Time. The most common empowerment killer is lack of time. There's only a certain amount of time in a day. As much as we would like more, we cannot magically turn 24 hours into 30 or expect employees to have super-human stamina and require no sleep. In one hospital, a group of nurse supervisors added up everything they were supposed to do in a shift. It totaled 26 hours per day. Obviously, they didn't have time to help each other or to adjust their responses to different situations, let alone complete all of their tasks.

In a typical workday, there is a certain amount of time and effort that employees must devote to mission-critical work: tending to patients, providing service to customers, working on a manufacturing line, answering phone calls, and closing sales. Employees use any time left over for meetings, reports, filling out forms, reading e-mail, or handling other administrative tasks. That leftover time is the *administrative task capacity* of a job or function. Very few organizations know what that capacity is, much less how to manage to it.

As tasks get added, they start to fill up that leftover time. In highly territorial environments, the amount of time employees need for administrative tasks tends to exceed the amount of time they need for mission-critical work, especially *empowered* mission-critical work when employees do more than check a box and move on. Moreover, stripping employees' empowerment by taking away time has serious consequences on the organization as a whole. For companies that pay employees by the hour, overtime pay results in dramatically higher labor costs. Lack of time can also take a huge toll on energy, quality, engagement, and morale for all employees.

Mission-critical work should always take priority over administrative tasks. But in territorial environments, it rarely does. So what suffers is what's most important. And territorial managers maintain control, even though this excess administrative burden may directly hurt a company's ability to achieve its overall mission.

To address this problem, organizations must determine what the administrative task capacity for a particular function actually is. The formula is quite simple: total number of work hours minus the number of hours that employees should spend on mission-critical work that benefits the organization. Determining the mission-critical time requirement is fairly easily for customer-facing roles that have clear expectations about the amount of time employees spend serving customers and for manufacturing roles that have a set amount of time scheduled to produce the forecasted amount of product.

While it can be somewhat trickier to determine the amount of time required for mission-critical work in other functions, every role produces something for someone. Ask employees how much time they spend doing their job well and meeting their responsibilities — and how much more time they need to maximize their contribution toward the success of the overall organization. Most employees can tell you how much time they need.

Once you know that time capacity, prioritize tasks based on the overall business. A software company found that its technical support personnel were spending so much time on special projects that they were unable to handle all of their primary responsibilities. So the company put a new group in place to evaluate the impact of proposed initiatives on the overall business before they were implemented, which made the problem much less acute.

Training opportunities. It's great to tell employees that they are empowered to do something. But it's meaningless if they don't know how to do it. Withholding or limiting training opportunities is a common and subtle way to preserve territorialism. A manager can say that all employees are empowered to learn how to work in another area, but if they can't obtain the required training, then those opportunities exist in name only.

Managers can restrict internal training by simply not offering opportunities, by limiting space, or by keeping a too-small travel budget. And even when travel costs are not an issue, a manager might say that she can't afford for an employee to be gone for even one day — even though having more highly skilled staff would eventually make the company more successful.

This limitation of empowerment applies not only to internal training, but also to continuing education. If a manager has a particularly valuable employee, he may be hesitant to support that employee's efforts to get an advanced degree or a higher level of certification because the manager may lose the employee or be forced to increase compensation. In one consumer goods manufacturing company, an exceptional analytical chemist started taking classes toward a chemical engineering degree. Once she completed that degree, she could be promoted to a different department. However, on days when she had class, her manager would routinely drop a ton of additional work on her desk at the last minute, effectively preventing her from getting to class. Shortly thereafter, she quit.

Managers should certainly justify training opportunities, and the staff member requesting the training should be able to show how getting the training will benefit the organization as a whole. But giving territorial managers the ability to decide *subjectively* who does and does not get training allows them to build territorial walls. Training criteria should be as objective as possible. And companies should expect and encourage managers to ensure that their staff continues to learn and grow.

Access to information or resources. Another way territorial managers can limit empowerment is by blocking access to information or resources that employees need. If employees can't access shipping information, they can't help customers track their orders. If they can't get to pricing information, they can't facilitate a sale. If they can't retrieve product availability information, they can't tell customers if their order will be filled.

Sometimes a department doesn't have the information, although the manager could get it. Sometimes the information is available, but frontline employees are not permitted to see it or communicate it to someone who needs it, all because a territorial manager wants to maintain control. Legal restrictions that mandate limits on information sharing are not barriers; they're just a part of the operating environment. But when information *could* be shared but *isn't* because of territorialism, the organization suffers.

Another way to restrict information is to prohibit employees from releasing or sharing the information they do have with employees outside their department, for no better reason than territorialism. Territorial departments are not willing to share their agendas or strategies with other departments. This information hoarding problem becomes especially prevalent around budget time. A key indicator of information hoarding is the assertion that other departments would misuse the information. Sometimes that may be true. But unless there is a legal or regulatory reason to restrict information, those who control it should be held accountable for making sure that the value of the information is maximized by everyone who needs it.

In one college, an entire department exists to produce reports on alumni donation records and projections on future contributions. That information is critical to almost everyone in the college's advancement operation. Producing these reports is easily automated, and there are numerous companies that can do it inexpensively. But when a new vice president suggested producing the reports off-site, the entire reporting department reacted in fury, insisting that the information was too confidential to be entrusted to outsiders (though all of it was public record), that the advancement team would mess up their system (though it was already riddled with inaccuracies), and that switching to another system would take too long (though the advancement team was already stymied by lack of information).

The reporting department turned this situation into a political battle that forced everyone on staff, even faculty, to take sides. It became such a debacle that the college's president refused to discuss the situation further, fearing more dissent and disruption. The college ended up spending a fortune paying a few people to do a job poorly and lost a substantial amount of money in potential contributions, all because the reporting department so thoroughly hoarded the alumni reporting information.

Organizations should determine information and resource rights based on need. If someone needs information to help make the organization more successful, then those who possess the information should have an incentive to share it. If the need is for training, then training should be provided. If the information is so technical that it requires specialized support, then that specialized support should be provided on a shared services basis, where those who provide the support are organized around and held accountable for meeting the needs of internal customers.

Unfortunately, in some organizations, there's no incentive to share information. After all, knowledge is power, and the more information someone controls, the more budget, authority, respect, and importance the keeper of knowledge may accumulate, even if doing so makes the organization less successful overall. A culture of information sharing should be a deliberate strategy, along with rewards for sharing and penalties for hoarding.

One accounting company came up with a uniquely clever way of making sure that information spreads throughout the company: All of its accountants have a blog. Not only can other employees access these blogs, but customers can also access some of them. These blogs support the company's brand of having employees who are extremely knowledgeable, and the very existence of the blogs is a catalyst for sharing information.

Employee participation and innovation. An employee has a great idea. It could save the company millions or bring in a huge account. But because she is a frontline employee, her voice is not heard. Her opinion does not count. It happens all the time. In one manufacturing facility, it was an unwritten rule that anyone in a plant uniform was simply not taken seriously. In another organization, the "innovation program" that employees could use to suggest ideas was a bottomless pit where suggestions simply vanished.

Some progressive organizations have developed effective innovation programs by recognizing that those closest to the action are most likely to see what will or will not work and may help find ways to make things run better. At Loma Linda University Health System, about 100 employees worked in four teams (about 25 people each) to develop hundreds of changes to improve the patient experience. This project, called "Innovating Excellence," resulted in significant improvement in patient satisfaction.

But companies have more immediate needs as well. Leaders and managers must be able to quickly act on an employee's innovative suggestion to solve a problem. If they do act on the employee's suggestion, not only can they solve the problem, but they can also increase employee engagement. One of the 12 key dimensions of employee engagement is "At work, my opinions seem to count." When employees believe that their opinions count, they are much more likely to be engaged. And if the workforce is engaged, the organization will likely see stronger profits, better productivity, lower turnover, fewer safety incidents, and stronger customer engagement.

Lack of access to information is a barrier to downward information flow (from those who have the information to those who need it). When employees' opinions don't count, that is a barrier to upward information flow (from the front line to those in authority). But the basic issue is the same. Managers across departments should be sharing. Employees should be able to get the answers or approval they need when they need it. Mapping the communication flow in an organization can shed light on where information is flowing well, where it is blocked, where it is vulnerable, and where it is too many layers removed. It's easy to visually map and diagnose communication flow using tools like social network analysis. Creating a visual map of communication links is an excellent way to demonstrate how robust a network is — or could be.

Managerial support. Even when all other barriers to empowerment have been removed, there's still a chance that efforts to empower employees will fail. If a manager does not support employees having some degree of freedom, then they really don't have freedom at all. As one sales representative put it, "I still have the boot mark in the back of my head from the last time I made a suggestion."

This particular aspect of disempowerment is perhaps the most difficult to deal with, mainly because a big part of the equation is the manager's talent mix. A highly talented manager who enjoys seeing her people grow and develop will encourage employees to spread their wings and will applaud them for it. A less talented manager will convince himself that his employees know less than he does and therefore can't be trusted to make any decisions, whether employees are "officially" allowed to or not.

In many companies, people are promoted to management to reward them for their performance, regardless of whether or not they have management talent. For most people, success as an individual contributor is because of their particular style, which may not lend itself to managing; someone might excel in a frontline role but have little to no managerial talent. Certainly, knowledge and experience are important. However, being a manager of people should not necessarily be more prestigious or lucrative than being a subject-matter expert. People should become managers because that's what they do best. People should become specialized experts if that's what they do best.

In one call center, the only way to reward employees who became good at what they did was to promote them. Over time, this resulted in six different layers of management to reward the best customer service representatives. Ultimately, if an employee was absolutely great at dealing with customers, she could become as much as six times removed from ever having to talk to a customer again.

Overcoming the barrier of promoting the wrong people may require revamping the leadership selection process to include a talent component. It may even require alternate career paths that allow people to grow personally and professionally in the area of what they do best. Google retains employees by rewarding them with greater freedom, including the company's rule that allows engineers and developers to spend 20% of their time working on their own personal projects (many of which have become successful Google products). This 20% rule includes a weekly peer review process in which employees evaluate each other's personal work. This sort of social pressure keeps quality high and encourages people to do what they do best.

By making sure that people's roles are matched with their talents while keeping all of the other aspects of empowerment in place, it becomes less likely that someone with territorial ambitions will surface, much less succeed. However, organizations must take care to ensure that a different set of barriers doesn't arise. As noted earlier, high levels of empowerment without accountability can damage an organization by creating Loose Cannons. Once employees are truly empowered, then that empowerment must be tempered by appropriate levels of accountability.

Accountability is not just the requirement to act a certain way or to accomplish specific tasks; it only truly exists when it is measurable and objective. Subjective accountability opens the door to accusations of unfairness, inconsistency, and inaccuracies in performance appraisals. Objective accountability that is based on clear and regularly reported metrics is not open to interpretation. The numbers speak for themselves. Performance criteria must, however, be the right metrics for the role. Essentially, metrics should fairly encompass what the job requires, have clear and achievable targets, and be reported regularly. They should be translated into different performance targets and applied with "procedural justice": The evaluation process should be fair, consistent, and without bias.

It's not unusual for companies to revamp their performance management system when they change employees' empowerment levels. In fact, it's a good idea to at least audit the current process to make sure it supports the overall objectives without creating additional barriers. And most importantly, these metrics should take into account the impact on the broader organization's mission and the associated desired outcome — not just what happens within a particular department.

Holding all employees accountable for the overall success of the organization and empowering them to succeed in furthering these objectives, including placing them with a talented manager, can help prevent territorial behavior from reaching a critical mass. If left unchecked, however, territorialism can spread like an epidemic. Once one group starts acting in a territorial manner, others may feel compelled to follow suit in an attempt to achieve their own goals. And when a department believes its control over its ability to succeed is threatened by the territorialism of another, it may start empire building, the third level of bureaucracy.

Overcoming these challenges is not a simple matter. It can be done, but only if rules, empowerment, and accountability are fixed first. Once that happens and parochialism and territorialism are reined in, then the organization can move on to the next phase: toppling empires.

Chapter Eight:

OVERCOMING EMPIRE BUILDING

Empire building — attempts to seize control over something that others control or share — is often a defensive response to the territorialism of another department. For instance, if one department is not sharing information that other departments need, another department may feel compelled to collect, compile, and store a duplicate database of its own. Consequently, one of the best ways to prevent empire building is to overcome territorialism.

However, that might not be enough. Once it creeps into existence, empire building may become too pervasive to conquer without some interventions of its own. The first step to overcoming empire building is to understand where it is occurring and why. Empire-building departments typically try to gain control in four areas:

- information
- budget and resources
- decision rights
- supervisory rights

Information. By attempting to seize control of information sources or developing a duplicate database, a department manager may believe she is restoring her group's self-sufficiency. However, if it makes more sense for the information to remain either in the public domain or where it currently resides, then making that type of shift is unlikely to benefit the overall organization.

Requesting or demanding information can also be an act of empire building. For example, a department may mandate reports, training, or meetings that others must attend or send out a barrage of memos and e-mails that push its own agenda. In one hospital, there were so many people trying to control what the nurses did during their shifts that one nurse manager just gave up: "I just print out all my e-mails, and if two weeks go by without anyone yelling at me about one of them, I just throw them out."

Information, even floods of it, is fine if the reports and meetings have a clear purpose and ultimately benefit the company without interfering with mission-critical work. Controlling or demanding information leads to empire building when the purpose of the desire to control becomes disconnected from the greater strategy of the organization and is only meant to further the influence and self-sufficiency of a particular department.

One national retailer had so many memos, meetings, initiatives, and conference calls that store managers were left with almost no time to run their stores. The problem grew one request at a time from different parts of the company but accumulated to create what became known as the "process tsunami." The company did not deliberately create this "tsunami." It was a flood of well-intentioned acts, but they were constructed in response to the fear of not having that one piece of information that a department thought it must have. That was all well and good until all of the seemingly small requests added up. Although those making the requests felt their self-sufficiency was restored, the store managers could no longer do their job. The wave drowned them.

Generally, companies create information assimilation barriers with the best of intentions. But ultimately, too much uncoordinated information is a subtle, but effective, form of empire building — it ensures that one voice is heard above all others.

Budget and resources. As business becomes more complex, allocating budget and resources becomes less and less objective. At some point, it's simply impossible to honor every request, no matter how worthy. Companies have to prioritize, and unfortunately, that directly threatens the self-sufficiency of those who lose the argument. That loss of self-sufficiency can lead to empire building, and one group might attempt to directly or indirectly take resources from another group. These resources are often financial, but they can also be things like office space, parking privileges, computer equipment, access to specialized resources, or even control over a conference room.

For one organization, it was ceiling tiles. This Fortune 100 company allocated office space according to pay grade level, and space was defined by the number of square-foot ceiling tiles in each office. When one manager was promoted, he insisted that he get the number of ceiling tiles he deserved, even though the floor was not large enough to accommodate every manager's approved amount. After escalating the issue all the way to top leadership, the company rebuilt the entire floor at a huge expense so the manager could get one more row of ceiling tiles — even though that meant others would have to give up office space they had, and deserved, based on their pay grade level.

Decision rights. Decision rights are all about who makes the call. Who decides if a pricing exception can be made or if a product campaign should go forward or if everyone should use the same reporting template? Who decides timelines and dates for deliverables, and who can make exceptions? Who has ultimate responsibility and thus authority? A lot of times, it's someone else. Some managers find that threatening.

Sometimes reallocating decision rights is the appropriate thing to do, such as allowing sales reps to make more decisions about their customers. But if there is no clear benefit to the company, managers seizing the decision rights of others could be driven by politics and a desire to expand their power base. If there isn't a valid business reason to change decision authority, then this sort of power play is a form of empire building.

A member of the marketing staff of a consumer products company had an idea for a new product. The company sold ammonia-based cleaner and vinegar-based cleaner. His idea was to combine the two solutions into a new product that contained both active ingredients. Such a product could corner the market, or so he thought. The company's chemists, upon hearing about this idea, told the marketing manager that they could not do it. Vinegar is an acid, and ammonia is a base. If they're combined, they form a type of salt water, which is not only totally useless, but the precipitate could clog the manufacturing lines. The marketing manager was able to get the authority to force the chemists to comply and mix up a large-scale batch anyway. As a result, "salt" was formed and clogged up the lines and machinery in the plant. The plant had to be shut down for several weeks so that the lines could be flushed out, which cost a significant amount of money and lost production time.

Supervisory rights. This form of empire building is all about who controls what other people do, particularly who has supervisory rights or management responsibilities. Should service be a separate organization, or should it be a support function to sales? Should IT be a shared service, or should it be part of operations?

Lobbying to take over another department is probably the most obvious kind of empire building. But it can take subtle forms: One group might attempt to take control over others' tasks on a particular operation or to be named account managers or project leaders. In many cases, that's fine because the buck has to stop somewhere. But when seizing control serves one department at the expense of another or at the expense of larger success, then it is a form of empire building.

Guiding principles. Shifts in control can be harmful — or the right decision. To figure out which, organizations have to apply the correct decision calculus. Is there an established, objective, and clear way to make the call, or is the decision based on fear and politics?

First, determine if you can justify centralizing information, resources, or decision/supervisory rights or if there is a legitimate need for a shift in authority to a different department. If it makes more sense for Department X to "own" something than it does for Department Y to continue to own it, then it should be moved to Department X. But if it makes more sense to keep it with Department Y, then Department Y needs to have some accountability for meeting Department X's needs. Department Y needs some skin in the game such as a shared goal or having its performance judged by internal customer surveys. If a particular group is named the custodian of certain information, that group needs to be held accountable for making sure the users of that resource have what they need in a timely manner and with adequate support. To help prevent political battles over allocating a resource, there should be as much responsibility in dispensing the resource as there is power in owning it.

Distributing resources becomes tricky when there are more requests than there are resources. That's why companies should base their solutions to the different types of empire building on an objective assessment of each situation using a set of guiding principles. These guiding principles can help organizations prioritize various courses of action according to what's best for the company. As with a rules audit, the decision to grant ownership or control should be based on one or more of the following:

- improving financial performance
- improving the workplace
- strengthening customer relationships
- limiting liability
- avoiding catastrophic failure

The scope of evaluation should apply to the total organization, not just one department. One construction equipment sales organization had a strict, limited cell phone reimbursement policy, even though its sales reps served dealers across wide territories. The accounting department insisted on this policy and maintained control of the rules regarding cell phone usage. When it became apparent that salespeople simply stopped selling once they reached their maximum reimbursement level, the company changed the policy. As a result, representatives were more willing to make additional calls to check in on their customers. *The guiding principle of doing what was best for customers and financial success trumped the accounting department's need for excessive control.*

Not everyone will be happy with the outcome of an overthrown empire, but at least overall success won't take a back seat to local success. If a decision does not have a clear and credible expected benefit to financial or workplace performance, legal issues, customer relationships, or the avoidance of serious trouble, it probably is not a good decision. If the decision simply exchanges one set of problems for another or appeases a desire for power, then ultimately, the change will cost the organization more than it's worth.

Short-term thinking. Decisions that foster empire building are typically a result of short-term thinking. One type of short-term thinking is a *sin of omission,* when decisions are made for short-term benefit without a full realization of the ultimate effect. A sin of omission is a barrier created by a hasty decision or a badly planned move, such as pulling resources off one project to save another, making it impossible for the first project to succeed. This becomes a problem when there is collateral damage to the broader organization.

When executives from Ford, Chrysler, and GM took private planes to Washington, D.C. to ask Congress for bailout funds, they did so because it was company policy. Their sin of omission was neglecting to consider how it would diminish their credibility. Another example: A company cuts a staff position to save money, but winds up paying twice as much in quality defects. Or an organization doesn't implement an IT plan because it seemed too costly, but without it, productivity declined.

Another type of short-term thinking is a *sin of commission*, when people fully realize that there will be long-term consequences, but they sweep those concerns under the rug. For example, a hiring freeze until product demand increases — even though the six-month learning curve leaves the company six months behind the market, or buying CDOs (collateralized debt obligations) at the top of the market — as Lehman Brothers did — even though warnings of doom were circulating through the company. When unpleasant consequences are well-known but brushed aside, dismissed, or minimized until it's too late, organizations are creating a sin of commission.

To avoid these types of problems, organizations should evaluate the guiding principles based on long-term *and* short-term impact on business success. Companies can't ignore the short term; doing so could put them out of business. But ultimately, the most important thing is the long term. Organizations will be better off making decisions that carefully consider long-term outcomes.

That's how Douglas Conant saved Campbell Soup Company. When he became CEO in 2001, the stock price was down, and the company wasn't meeting earnings expectations. Campbell had been the poorest performing of all major global food companies for years. The workforce was disengaged, and there was good reason to believe that the company would soon go on the block.

Conant knew he had to make some drastic decisions that would have an impact on Campbell right away and for the long haul, and he had to make them immediately. His first order of business was firing 300 of his top 350 people. "We had 20,000 people working for those 300 executives who were miserable," Conant said in an interview with the *Gallup Management Journal*. "You want to deal with your global leadership team in a thoughtful, caring, responsible way. But on the other hand, you're accountable to 20,000 employees who are looking to you for leadership and who are anticipating for things to change — and so were our external stakeholders."

That move made 20,000 people happier, and it also wrecked a lot of silos. In the short term, the move was great for morale, and the long-term benefit was 300 new leaders who shared Conant's precise vision for the future. As he put it, "You can't win in the marketplace unless you first win in the workplace." So he and the leadership team enacted measures to improve employee engagement, innovation, and productivity. These measures had a positive short-term effect, but they also drove the company's long-term goal of building "the world's most extraordinary food company by nourishing people's lives everywhere, every day."

All of those short-term decisions cost something: time, energy, money, 300 jobs. A lot of people didn't like them, and few were certain they would work. But each of these decisions showed a long-term return on investment that more than made up for the cost: Campbell is now an industry leader, its investors are happy, and its workforce is engaged.

"As people get engaged, they get engaged in more than just their departments," said Conant. "They start getting engaged in the enterprise, and they have conversations with each other about how the company can move forward, not about how IT moves forward or how supply chain moves forward. . . . When you're engaged in trying to do something special to lift the entire company up, all of a sudden the conversations change. People feel more accountable to each other, and they don't want to let each other down."

Chapter Nine:
COURAGE ENABLERS

Imagine a work environment where employees spend their entire careers being controlled by parochial or territorial managers. These employees have learned that empowerment is a pipe dream and that the only way to survive is to obey direction without question. Joe, the customer service manager from Chapter One, didn't have to imagine such an environment — he lived it. If the leaders of companies like Joe's were to identify and remove the internal barriers that create and sustain harmful bureaucracy in their organizations, the employees would be free to spread their wings and start to make decisions of their own. But if the enterprising people who try are run out of the company, few others will have the courage to take risks.

Removing barriers is only the first step. Leaders must give employees the encouragement, energy, commitment from above, and support to try new things and to focus on the greater good of the overall organization. Leaders need to give special attention to courage enablers to ensure that new barriers aren't built. Once rules, empowerment, accountability, information flow, and resources have all been addressed, managers need to foster courageous behavior through four types of actions:

- aligning vital courage and moral courage
- matching responsibilities with strengths
- engaging employees
- rewarding courageous behavior

Aligning vital courage and moral courage. Shane Lopez and the late C.R. Snyder are perhaps the foremost experts in research regarding hope and courage. They defined three types of courage. Two apply particularly well to organizations: *vital courage* and *moral courage*. Vital courage is the "inspiration for actions that improve one's lot in life or that ultimately promote survival." Moral courage is "the authentic expression of one's beliefs or values in pursuit of justice or the common good despite power differentials, dissent, disapproval, or rejection." While vital courage is inwardly focused (survival), moral courage is outwardly focused (ideology). Vital courage is about what's best for the employee. Moral courage is about what's best for the organization.

Examples of vital courage include when an employee takes a risk or does something extraordinary to further his own standing in the company. Taking these actions may limit his personal time or cause difficulty in his normal day-to-day routine. But the intent of the courageous activity is "what's in it for me?" In its benevolent form, vital courage might include working an extra shift, writing a new proposal, or taking night courses to qualify for a raise. Though these actions further an individual goal, they also help the organization accomplish its overall mission. But in its malevolent form, vital courage may lead to gaming a bonus, manipulating data, scheming against colleagues, or stabbing others in the back. Essentially, the difference between the benevolent and malevolent forms of vital courage is whether the actions benefit the greater purpose of the organization or benefit only individual employees or their departments.

In Enron's final years, the company made destructive vital courage an implied corporate value. Few, if any, departments reported accurate information; employees were encouraged to undermine each other; and those who reported the best numbers — by means fair or, more commonly, foul — were richly rewarded. This kind of corrupted courage led directly to the company's collapse.

Moral courage manifests in the workplace when an employee takes a risk or goes the extra mile — not necessarily because it benefits him personally, but because it's best for the organization. The clerk who stops what he's doing to help an elderly customer around the store even though it will make it more difficult to complete his other tasks on time is showing moral courage. The employee who jumps in to help a coworker, even though it may mean working late to complete her daily responsibilities is displaying moral courage.

In barrier-plagued companies, employees may be expected to display moral courage *at the expense of* vital courage. The problem is, vital courage usually wins. Employees might display vital courage by resisting the urge to take a risk or to make a decision because doing so might result in them losing their job. When faced with the choice between doing what is best for the company while creating harm for yourself versus improving your lot in life regardless of the impact on others, many will choose the latter. As noted in Chapter Two, George Loewenstein found that people tend to alter their definitions of right and wrong based on what is personally best for them. Consider the following situations based on real-life examples from a financial services company.

Managers in Company A were evaluated and paid based on the average production per hour of their team members. Once frontline employees met certain internal requirements, they were technically eligible to enter a "development pool" for additional training and eventual assignment as a manager. Assignment to the pool was considered a promotion.

George was a leader in this company, and he was asked to nominate someone to enter the development pool. He nominated his best performer who also had, in George's opinion, the most management talent. After that person left his group, his team's average production declined. After all, he'd lost his best performer. As a result,

George's pay declined sharply, and he received a poor performance review.

Sherry was the leader of a second group and was also asked to nominate someone to enter the development pool. She chose her worst performer who could not even manage himself much less other reps. But, as a result, once that person left the group, Sherry's pay increased sharply because her average had gone up (now that the poor performer was no longer there to drag the group down), and she received a glowing performance review for improving her numbers.

George decided to display moral courage by doing what was best for the company, even though he suffered as a result. Sherry, on the other hand, chose to exhibit vital courage by looking out for herself, regardless of what was best for the company. Neither scenario is good; both are guaranteed to fail. If employees are forced to choose between what's best for themselves and what's best for the organization, then the organization will never overcome its fear-based barriers.

Leaders need to make employees feel comfortable *and motivated* to perform acts of moral courage. The key is to design rewards and performance management in a way that balances and aligns both types of courage. When vital courage and moral courage coexist and are in alignment, then employees will be rewarded when they do something that benefits themselves as well as the organization as a whole — and face consequences when they harm overall success.

In the previous example, if the managers had received a bonus if the person they nominated was successful, then in both cases, the right person would probably have been nominated. Neither George nor Sherry would have suffered as a result. In fact, a different company in the same industry was faced with the same dilemma, and it solved the problem by giving the referring supervisor a bonus if the person nominated for promotion met his or her first-year goals. As a result, only those with strong management talent were promoted, and the referring supervisors were compensated for the temporary decline in their numbers.

Any time an organization introduces a new policy, program, incentive, or bonus scheme, leaders and managers should ask themselves if moral and vital courage align or conflict. When there is conflict between the moral and vital instincts of the employee, failure is sure to follow, and leaders should take immediate action to correct the situation. There is, however, one important caveat to keep in mind: Moral courage should always be focused on the organization or the desired outcome and not the successful completion of just one part of the process. Otherwise, an organization runs the risk of creating an entirely new wave of parochialism.

Matching responsibilities with strengths. Different jobs require different talents. For employees to excel and use their talents to adapt to new situations, they must have the innate ability to do so. This may seem obvious, but all too often, organizations move people into positions without regard for their individual talents. In fact, in many companies, the only way up is through a management role, which penalizes those who are more talented as individual contributors than as managers. They're taken out of roles they are well-suited for and given roles in which they're weak. Furthermore, management shouldn't be a prize for performance. Managing people is simply another job that should be filled by those with talents that fit that role. But that is some employees' only hope of progress — and the company thinks that training will fill in what the employees lack.

It usually won't. Training is fine for skills and knowledge gaps, but it can't create talent where talent doesn't exist. In fact, research has shown that developing an underused talent results in a much greater performance improvement than trying to turn a weakness into a strength. Moreover, if employees are expected to perform tasks that they struggle with, they are likely to avoid risks and to underperform.

In a highly territorial environment, employees may lack the freedom to discover their own career path. But companies can find ways to allow people to grow in their role. Thought leaders, subject-matter experts, coaches, and innovation specialists are just a few examples of career paths that companies can create for highly talented high-performing workers whose talents exist outside of management.

Organizations that effectively create individualized career paths for talented employees have seen dramatic benefits. One heavy equipment manufacturer began to use a strengths-based approach to determine eligibility for a fast-track manager training program. The failure rate for those going through the program dropped from an unacceptably high level to virtually zero within six months.

Engaging employees. As mentioned earlier, employee engagement is strongly linked to business performance. Engaged workers generate more profit, create stronger customer relationships, have fewer safety incidents, are less likely to quit, and are more productive than disengaged workers. Engagement provides the energy that fuels a workplace. A talented and engaged employee in a barrier-free workplace with a supportive manager is likely to excel.

Managers are the fulcrum of engagement. While barriers that lead to harmful bureaucracy are generally created incrementally all over the company, engagement is created locally between one manager and one employee. That's why there can be — and often are — extreme variances in engagement and performance among workgroups within the same company. Talented managers engage their people, and untalented managers don't. Many companies have workgroups in the 90th percentile of engagement as well as workgroups in the 10th percentile, compared to Gallup's overall database of engagement. In essence, a company can have as many cultures as it has workgroups.

Breaking down fear-based barriers can reduce this variance. Why? Because barriers inhibit engagement. However, just because the pyramid of bureaucracy has been destroyed doesn't mean employees will necessarily become engaged. There may still be local issues unique to each workgroup. But when the barriers are removed and employees have greater freedom, companies can effectively and promptly address these local issues. It's much easier to bring an organization to a consistent level of high engagement once bureaucracy has been tamed.

Because engagement is essentially a local phenomenon, leaders must measure and manage it locally. As one healthcare consultant said, "When you bake a cake, you need equal heat from the top and the bottom to make it come out right. Removing barriers at the enterprise level is the heat from the top. Engaging employees locally is the heat from the bottom." The key to measuring and managing employee engagement at the local workgroup level is to focus on the aspects of engagement that strongly relate to ultimate business success. As mentioned earlier, Gallup's employee engagement assessment, the Q^{12}, is comprised of 12 items that measure the 12 critical aspects of engagement that have been proven to propel business success. These items are:

- I know what is expected of me at work.

- I have the materials and equipment I need to do my work right.

- At work, I have the opportunity to do what I do best every day.

- In the last seven days, I have received recognition or praise for doing good work.

- My supervisor, or someone at work, seems to care about me as a person.

- There is someone at work who encourages my development.

- At work, my opinions seem to count.

- The mission and purpose of my company makes me feel my job is important.

- My fellow employees are committed to doing quality work.

- I have a best friend at work.

- In the last six months, someone at work has talked to me about my progress.

- This last year, I have had opportunities at work to learn and grow.

Measuring and managing these items locally while removing organizational barriers can unlock the potential of all employees and increase employee engagement. Engaged employees are good for business: In a financial services company, higher levels of engagement meant stronger productivity. In a manufacturing firm, greater engagement resulted in fewer accidents. In a hospital, increased engagement led to improvements in patient outcomes and safety rates. Other businesses saw increased sales, lower turnover, better customer relationships, and higher market share. What all of these organizations found is that engaged employees are a prerequisite for courage *and* success. Once people are willing, able, and allowed to be courageous, the next step is to reward them for their courageous behavior.

Rewarding courageous behavior. When transformational change occurs in an organization, some will immediately adopt the new system, but others will wait and see.

Both responses are sensible. The organization has most likely attempted a multitude of "culture changes" that it abandoned when push came to shove — often because of resistance from parochial and territorial managers. So to get more people to try things the new way and embrace change, reward the brave few who take the first tentative steps.

The reward doesn't have to be a trophy or a bonus; it could be a note from a manager, a pat on the back, or a story told at a department meeting. Whatever the vehicle, leaders should reinforce and celebrate courageous behavior. And the reward should be meaningful to the person you are rewarding and clearly linked to the types of new behaviors you are seeking. For example, if a group is trying to increase empowerment and an employee finds a new way to fix an old problem within established guidelines, then treat him like a hero — and make the celebration meaningful for him.

When Tommy Lasorda was managing the Los Angeles Dodgers, the team usually stayed at a Marriott in Atlanta when they were playing the Braves. Albert "Smitty" Smith was a bellhop at Marriott. Smitty generally was on shift when the Dodgers arrived and got to know Lasorda well. One day when the Dodgers were in town, Smitty found out that they were staying in a different hotel and took it upon himself to meet Lasorda at the other hotel — wearing a full Dodgers uniform — and let him know that if the game ran late, he would bring over Lasorda's special "late-night snack" afterward because the other hotel's food service would be closed. As a result, the

Dodgers switched back to staying at the Marriott. The hotel benefited from Smitty's display of moral courage, and he was rewarded. He went on to become a sports ambassador for the Marriott Marquis and was inducted into the Atlanta Convention & Visitors Bureau Hospitality Hall of Fame in 1999.

In the end, by focusing on aligning moral and vital courage; matching responsibilities with strengths; engaging employees; rewarding courageous behavior; and aggressively rooting out parochialism, territorialism, and empire building, a company will have almost everything it needs to be fearless. There is one more thing to watch out for: courage killers.

Chapter Ten:
BEWARE OF COURAGE KILLERS

Organizations that have become technically barrier free may not be truly free. If a culture is to genuinely change, employees must have the courage and the support to take advantage of their newfound freedoms. Certainly, removing barriers that lead to bureaucracy and creating an environment that enables courageous behavior are both necessary, but that's not enough. Fear can still crush a company's ability to succeed through courage killers — lingering behaviors and actions that prevent courageous behavior from taking hold.

Managers who lack the talent to do their job effectively are at the source of many courage killers. After all, it is easier to intimidate subordinates than to inspire them — especially if the manager fears losing control. Low-talent managers may feel there is no other way to maintain their position. There are many ways for these managers to discourage courageous behavior in an organization. Some of the more common courage killers are:

- inconsistency
- playing the blame game
- hoarding information
- public floggings
- subjectivity/rewarding subservience over service
- excessive control

Inconsistency. This pervasive evil can take many forms. A manager might praise one employee but sternly punish someone else for doing essentially the same thing. When one employee is allowed to get away with something, but others are not, it sends a clear message that there are no rules, only moods and shades of favor. The implication is that if you offend the boss, he will find a way to make you pay for it.

Inconsistency doesn't have to involve more than one person, though. Managers who are unpredictable and react differently to similar situations for no apparent reason teach employees that they would be better off doing nothing on their own and should wait for explicit direction on what they should do next. This type of behavior is sure to restore a toppled bureaucracy.

To reduce inconsistency and create courageous behavior, organizations must have clear and objective rules that they communicate well and that everyone in the organization fully understands. They should enforce those rules as consistently as possible, based on hard outcome metrics rather than opinion. And organizations need to apply rewards and consequences fairly, transparently, and judiciously.

Playing the blame game. This courage killer tells workers that they are empowered *at their own risk*. If an employee succeeds, then taking a risk was fine. But failure results in recriminations, regardless of whether the employee has the support and blessing of his manager. One employee described the situation at his company as "Sick Sigma": Ideas that fail could cost people their career. There is learning in failure. If an idea fails, that failure can be used to help others come up with a better way, trigger a training opportunity, or otherwise identify what is or isn't effective. As Thomas Edison said, "I have not failed. I've just found 10,000 ways that won't work."

Of course, companies must have clear performance standards. Employees should not be empowered to do whatever they want, and they certainly shouldn't be rewarded for serious mistakes. But if an employee implements an idea or strategy that her manager supports and that falls within company guidelines, then she should not be blamed if things go wrong. Yes, the employee should participate in a thorough postmortem to discover why the idea failed, but the manager should never openly criticize her for taking a risk that the manager encouraged in the first place.

Managers who are not willing to support employees who are acting within the rules or with the manager's consent send a message that they cannot be trusted. Employees quickly conclude that it's safer to just not try anything new or different. Better yet, do as little as possible. But managers who publicly stand behind their employees and encourage intellectual energy and initiative are tremendously beneficial to their companies.

Interface, a billion-dollar soft-surfaced modular floor covering company, has a formal system in place to encourage its employees to take risks: the Play to Win team-building exercise. "Unless everyone learned to freely — even aggressively — question the status quo, to anticipate and embrace change, to identify opportunities, to be flexible and react quickly, there was no hope of becoming the kind of organization that might one day be the first sustainable corporation in history," wrote Interface's chairman Ray Anderson in his book *Confessions of a Radical Industrialist: Profits, People, Purpose — Doing Business by Respecting the Earth.* "[The Play to Win program] also encouraged people to move outside their comfort zones and let go of their old, established patterns of behavior. People were even given permission to fail, but to learn from failure and try again."

Hoarding information. To be empowered, employees must have access to the information and resources they need to do their jobs properly. One way that managers can discourage expressions of freedom among their staff is to withhold key pieces of information that only the manager is authorized to use or release. Hoarding information can build territorial walls and kill courage within those walls.

Of course, employees might not have access to information that is sensitive or regulated, when legal considerations apply. Hoarding information becomes a courage killer when non-regulated information such as policies, customer lists, pricing guidelines, or even parts availability *could* be released but isn't, mainly because the owner of that information is being territorial. In one sales organization, representatives weren't trusted with access to the customer information system, so they could not answer most of their customers' questions — including requests as simple as order status.

Hoarding information can kill courageous behavior by undermining empowerment, despite employees' intentions. If the manager makes every decision, then employees become instantly bound by that manager's desires. Business will proceed based on that manager's timeline, which may not always be in sync with business realities. Employees learn that the information barrier preventing them from breaking free of harmful bureaucratic practices is still very much in place, and there is nothing they can do about it.

Ultimately, unless there is a compelling legal or regulatory reason to keep information from employees, companies should not tolerate information hoarding. The speed of business depends, to a large extent, on the speed of information. If the flow is slowed or stopped, business is slowed or stopped. If the flow is fast and smooth, then businesses become responsive and adaptive. Managers who can't handle giving up that level of control probably shouldn't be managers.

Public floggings. A technical analyst in an industrial products company joined the organization with high hopes and expectations. However, her optimism was quickly dashed. When the manager of her workgroup was disappointed in an employee's performance, that manager would get an inch from the offending employee's face and scream at him in front of the entire group during meetings. After witnessing a few of these episodes, the new employee quit and took another job, even though the pay was lower.

Different types of work environments have different levels of acceptability for public criticism. But in most situations, it is not a good idea and will certainly kill courage, especially if the employee was trying to further an overall corporate goal and become less bureaucratic. If you do need to critique an employee, focus on performance outcomes or a clear violation of policy or ethics. If the employee did something that was technically right but made the manager look bad, then a coaching session on working as a team may be all you need. This should be a two-way dialogue that ultimately brings about the desired behavior without corroding the credibility of the group as a whole — not an excuse to demean and belittle the employee.

One progressive manager told an employee who was terribly upset after making a mistake, "I don't expect you to never make mistakes. If you never make mistakes, you never learn. If your intentions are good and you act within the rules, I will back you up. I do, however, expect you to not make the *same* mistake over and over again."

Subjectivity, or rewarding subservience over service. When organizations base performance metrics on clearly communicated and achievable targets that pertain to objective outcomes, then everyone knows exactly what they need to do. But when performance is determined subjectively, based on nothing more than a supervisor's opinion, an organization opens itself up to this courage killer.

A manager who is afraid of losing control might be tempted to give better reviews to "yes men" than to those who show more initiative, if doing so helps her maintain control. If organizations don't base recognition and advancement on objective customer and financial outcomes, then some managers may feel compelled to play favorites. General Motors' leadership used to be known for succession planning based on promoting "the unobvious choice." The method was intended to instill loyalty because promotion wasn't based on talent, performance, or even seniority: It was a reward for being "loyal" to one's superior.

If a manager makes it clear that he grants favor to those who don't question authority, don't resist change, or don't attempt to take advantage of new freedoms, then those freedoms don't really exist. If, on the other hand, evaluations are based on actual performance — either in terms of a more effective work environment, better financial outcomes, lower risk, or stronger customer relationships all while staying within policy guidelines — then it becomes harder for a manager's subjectivity to discourage courageous behavior.

One credit card company found a negative correlation between its internal subjective perceptions of customer service and what customers actually thought. In other words, what the company defined as good service was actually bad service, and vice versa. But the company assumed it was doing the right thing because the employees followed predetermined steps with perfect compliance. That, as it turned out, wasn't actually what customers wanted. When the company started letting customers rate their service encounter experiences and employees delivered on those expectations while still ensuring compliance with legal requirements and policy, service ratings skyrocketed.

It may not be appropriate to eliminate all subjective measures, especially if an employee doesn't work well with others on the team. And there are, of course, some roles that don't easily lend themselves to objective performance criteria. Ultimately, though, every group produces something for someone. Quantifying and measuring the benefit of what each group produces, even if it is internal, can help balance performance evaluation against subjective criteria. But leaders should consider these softer criteria in terms of ultimate measurable success and always view them in the context of the broader organizational goals. The mission and organizational success should always come first.

Excessive control. Imagine that you're a patient on the operating table and your heart suddenly stops beating. Would you want to wait for your doctors to get the OK from their department head to try to revive you? Of course not. Then why are so many companies willing to do that to their customers? It's not unusual for sales reps to have to get permission to release product status information to their customers or for employees to have to get sign-off before even buying a customer a cup of coffee.

Organizations must set ground rules for the types of decisions employees can make. And as long as employees stay within those parameters and there is some accountability for results, they should be free to make decisions. An environment that allows this type of freedom can completely change the relationship between employees and their managers. When managers make every decision, they essentially perpetuate a parent-toddler dynamic; employees often say such managers treat them "like children." But when employees are empowered to make decisions and they honor the ground rules, the manager becomes more of a coach, providing guidance on how to make the best decisions and focusing on helping employees learn how to improve.

Fear exists locally, and unless there is coordinated and irrevocable dedication to removing barriers and supporting courageous behavior within guidelines, some managers who fear giving up their current level of control may be tempted to subvert the process by putting up new barriers. For real change to occur, organizations must unite all managers in an absolute commitment to allow organizational needs to trump local needs. Accomplishing this transformation isn't easy. It may mean reassignment for leaders who cannot operate this way — especially during periods of change when everyone is watching to see if the change is real or simply the flavor of the month.

When organizations allow courage killers to exist, employees get a strong signal that change is in name only, and after a few months, things will go back to business as usual. If an organization attempts to implement change and fails, it will be much harder to succeed next time. In the end, it is critical for companies to aggressively root out and destroy any attempts to use courage killers to protect barriers. The consequences of failure can be severe: squandered resources, wasted opportunities, employee disengagement, and even ruined enterprises.

Chapter Eleven:

THE LEADERSHIP IMPERATIVE

There are no fearless leaders, but there are courageous ones. Everyone has fears they need to face. The key is to learn to overcome those fears. Mark Twain said, "Courage is resistance to fear, mastery of fear — not absence of fear." To create a fearless company, leaders must master fear — their own and others'. They have to have the courage to fix what's wrong.

The first fear leaders have to face is their own fear of loss. Step one is putting everything on the table. There should be no entitlements, endowments, policies, or practices that are exempt from examination, except those required by law. Leaders are just as prone to parochialism, territorialism, and empire building as anyone else, if not more so. And if they create barriers, they can't expect others in the organization not to do the same.

Once everything is out in the open and all past entitlements and barriers have been put aside, on a blank sheet of paper, the organization's leadership should craft a vision of what the company can become — not an impossible dream, but a realistic assessment of what the organization can accomplish if it defeats its fears, its barriers, and its nagging problems. Achieving that vision should be the mission of the organization.

Mission success must be the ultimate barometer of everything that happens in the organization. Anything that contributes to it should be encouraged; anything that detracts from or has an unknown relationship to mission success should be discouraged or eliminated. However, the mission is unlikely to succeed unless the entire leadership team aligns itself with the shared goal, and achieving that degree of unanimity takes work. The leader needs to present the vision and discuss it with each member of the senior team one by one. Members should have the opportunity to voice their concerns and objections. Some objections will be valid; some will not. The final judge and arbiter must *always* be mission success. The leader should embrace suggestions that further the mission; suggestions that don't are irrelevant background noise.

It may take a few days of wrangling and debating to get all of the concerns and potential conflicts aired. When that process is over, however, the leadership team *must* present a united front. Team members should have submitted, tried, and judged all concerns by then. As soon as the team has final decisions on all matters, team members need to be in perfect alignment. If members of the leadership team expect to hold their employees to a higher standard, they must hold themselves to the same, if not higher, standard. Those who cannot get on board and who cannot get behind the mission have no place on the leadership team and may need to find another role in the organization or elsewhere.

Once leadership has achieved agreement and alignment with the mission, the next step is to determine how each department and function companywide will contribute to mission success. Recognition, budgets, advancement, hiring strategies, and other decisions should start and end with mission. Every department must consider its role in these decisions as well as how it will support other departments.

Specific goals, budget allocation, and distribution of resources should be based on these guiding principles:

- improving financial performance
- improving the workplace
- strengthening customer relationships
- limiting liability
- avoiding catastrophic failure

These issues are best decided locally. The overall *direction* of the strategy, however, should be driven by leadership and based on mission.

One faith-based hospital chain created a set of corporate values that reflected the religious convictions of the institution's management and infused them throughout the entire organization. Unlike many organizations that try to adopt corporate values and find themselves touting meaningless phrases that are widely mocked, this hospital chain's simple value statements — such as "Dignity" and "Excellence" — became the ultimate arbiters, guideposts, and unifying threads that tied the entire organization together. The hospital chain made all decisions in the context of these values. It built recognition programs around them, as well as promotions, strategies, and even budgets. When conflicts arose, the values determined who won. Violations of the values were not tolerated, regardless of the offender's seniority. And when employees of all different functions and levels were asked what they would never want to change about the organization, the unanimous answer was "the values."

When leaders make decisions that determine budgets, recognition criteria, or performance targets, they directly or indirectly create a set of standards that others will generally follow. It is easy to try to enforce those standards through fear, but those who lead through fear will inspire fear. That fear will lead to barriers, and those barriers will inhibit success. While basing all decisions solely on mission — supported by objective, timely, and accurate metrics — doesn't eliminate fear, it does promote courage. Mission-centric decisions are less divisive and are inherently simplifying, permitting leaders to take a deep breath and judge the best way forward on a clear and powerful construct: If the mission fails, all fail. If the mission succeeds, all succeed. So if one group succeeds and the mission still fails, then in reality, no one succeeds.

An organization cannot become aligned around a unified mission by being reactive. Success won't come from directing employees' every move, thought, phrase, and activity; from checking everything everyone does before it leaves the department; or from dismissing any new idea as insubordinate. Good leaders are obsessively proactive. Leading means inspiring. It means setting the direction, making course corrections when necessary, defining success, and helping people thrive.

In the 1960s, President Kennedy said that the United States would put a man on the moon within a decade. At the time, doing so was more science fiction than science. However, aligned with that one mission, industry and academia alike rallied to create a wave of pride, motivation, and excitement that led to countless innovations, and eventually, as Neil Armstrong famously said, a "small step for man; one giant leap for mankind." If a leader inspires, aligns, motivates, and enables the organization around a common vision, then a company has taken the first step toward becoming fearless.

The second phase of the leadership imperative is mastering the fears of others. Enabling courage requires strong leadership support. Top and local leadership set the tone and values associated with enabling courage. To achieve a culture in which acting courageously in support of the mission is just the way the organization does business, leadership must show diligence, discipline, and direction. Success requires consistent commitment throughout the organization. Leadership should visibly recognize and reward those who achieve success while enabling courageous behavior.

At the same time, leadership should not tolerate any courage-killing behaviors. Leaders should make it absolutely clear that even if courage-killing behaviors happened in the past, they have no place in the future of the company. It will take vigilance and perhaps occasional interventions to head off emerging pockets of harmful bureaucracy — if left unchecked, the disease can spread quickly throughout the organization. This vigilance is not just top management's responsibility. Leaders of every rank need to set the right example, define how *their* team will contribute to the mission and the success of teams that they rely on or that rely on them, and determine how success will be measured.

Perhaps the most important way for leaders to manage the fears of others is to manage reference points. As noted in Chapter One, fear of loss does not necessarily come from an outcome itself, but rather from the reference point or expectation about that outcome. If a group achieves an outcome and that outcome is above the reference point, everyone is happy. If that outcome is below the reference point, loss aversion and fear may result. Falling short of a reference point on an outcome results in a sharp drop in value or utility, which is where fear of loss comes into play. So it's just as important to manage expectations about outcomes as it is to manage the outcomes themselves.

Part of the leadership imperative then becomes understanding who sets reference points, how they are set, and where there are conflicting versions. When reference points conflict, it is likely because of a parochial or territorial view in one or more parts of the organization. Conflicting reference points are dangerous because they send different signals about the same level of performance. In one case, the result may be engaged and happy employees. In another case, the result may be loss aversion because those who fall short of the reference point will have, in their minds, failed. If the reference points are aligned along the same outcomes, then the pieces of the puzzle should all fit together. If they are not aligned, harmful bureaucracy is likely to result. And then, once again, with the best of intentions, barriers are born.

Aligning reference points is not easy, and it requires constant attention. Because different groups look at the same initiative in different ways, there is a natural tendency to have different versions of success. Consider how a salesperson, customer service rep, human resources manager, IT programmer, and accountant view a customer promotion program. The salesperson will be most concerned with how much gets sold. The customer service rep will be most concerned with making sure the product works. The others will be more focused on productivity, cost, and efficiency. But the program is the same.

At one time, the management of Domino's Pizza set a reference point that all pizzas would be delivered in 30 minutes or less. At 31 minutes, the company and the customer considered the delivery to be a failure. On the other hand, if customers ordered pizza from the neighborhood pizza parlor, it was just fine if it came within 45 minutes. If it arrived in 31 minutes, they were thrilled. But if their Domino's pizza came in 31 minutes, they were disappointed. The reason for the difference in responses is nothing more than different reference points for the same outcome. The same dynamic applies for wages and bonuses, promotion criteria, headcount, budget, IT initiatives, marketing budgets, perks, time off, and business performance.

Overcoming fear and breaking down barriers to achieve organizational change may seem easiest when there is a crisis. But waiting for that to happen is not a good idea. Companies that make changes only during a crisis inevitably will make addressing the crisis the sole focus of the changes. What happens when the crisis is over? The motivation for the changes also comes to a screeching halt. We studied a hospital in the New York City area that was plagued with territorialism and barriers. Different departments did not get along, and conflict was rampant. However, immediately following the 9/11 terrorist attacks, all of those differences were put aside as the casualties came pouring in. Departments leapt to help each other and did what was necessary to take care of the victims and their families. But in the weeks that followed, despite the changes that the hospital made to deal with the horror of 9/11, each department crept back to its old way of doing things. And once again, conflict increased and cooperation eroded.

In our experience, companies that were able to effect the most lasting changes tore down barriers not in response to a crisis, but as part of an obsessive drive to constantly improve. One technical service organization created an entirely new program focused on excellence. The program included new levels of empowerment and a shift in focus from process to customers. The company created an elaborate recognition and celebration program all because of a quest to improve its level of service. Employees suddenly felt more valued, and the entire work environment became more energized. And as a result, independent evaluations of service quality improved to become one of the industry's best. The organization didn't make these changes in response to a crisis. The focus of the changes was simply a desire to be the best.

Breaking down barriers and creating a fearless company is not conditional or driven by events. It is a way of doing business that should permeate every aspect of an organization. It's easy to get people to be courageous during a crisis, and it certainly can provide a short-term catalyst for change. And yes, it takes a lot more work to be courageous during the normal daily grind. But courageous leadership and behavior need to happen every day for an organization to become free of harmful barriers. When that happens, a company can become truly fearless. If the company doesn't become fearless, fear will wreak its inevitable damage. As business consultant W. Edward Deming said, "It is not necessary to change. Survival is not mandatory."

Chapter Twelve:
THE FEARLESS COMPANY

Imagine a company where people in every department work together seamlessly, where employees are engaged and empowered to use their talents and strengths to do what's right. Imagine managers who work together toward a common goal, rather than against each other promoting their own local agendas. Imagine a company where rules protect against the bad, but don't prevent the good — where the ultimate barometer of right and wrong, have and have not, and recognition and reward is the success of the company as a whole. Imagine a company where fear of loss doesn't cause it to self-destruct. Imagine a company that is fearless. And then imagine the fear its competitors would feel.

Parochialism, territorialism, and empire building may seem like iron-clad barriers that cannot be torn down. But it is critical to remember that these walls were built internally, one brick at a time, out of fear. They weren't there when the company was started. They don't have to be there now.

If leaders are bold enough to see through the fear and dissect the root causes that make up this destructive pyramid of bureaucracy, they will see that these barriers can be overcome. Barriers that were built internally can be destroyed internally.

Barrier busting takes a great deal of courage. Executives and managers need to look in the mirror and say that absolutely everything is on the table. This will create tension and may cause some to leave. It can also mean the difference between success and failure. Removing barriers starts with understanding what people are trying to protect and shifting their reference points toward the greater good rather than local processes. Leaders should structure rules and policies to prevent walls from forming, instead of using them as the bricks and mortar that parochial managers need to build their dream castles.

As competition over resources increases, companies must take great care to manage the territorialism that will inevitably follow. Aggressively protecting empowerment, focusing on outcomes, and holding people accountable for the right things are absolutely critical to maintaining an open and collaborative environment. Organizations can limit empire building through better management of information, focusing on the long term, and having an outcomes-based resource prioritization process.

Company leaders must also properly manage information flow across departments to help ensure that they are enabling courageous behavior and that empowerment levels remain high. Information flow should be relevant and balanced: not enough information and people can't do their jobs; too much and mission-critical work will suffer as people become buried in e-mails, meetings, and memos.

Organizations can optimize resources by allocating them based on guiding principles that are focused on total company success rather than on one group's parochial or territorial attempts to trump another group. At the same time, leaders must beware of fear-based decisions that are focused on short-term needs rather than a long-term vision. Those decisions can lead to a reformation of the barriers that make up the pyramid of bureaucracy.

This journey can be difficult, challenging, exhilarating, and cathartic. It is a fundamentally emotional experience for the employees who finally have the chains of bureaucracy removed. Completing the journey is nothing less than a celebration of freedom and the first step on a path toward greater success, as was the case with Joe once barriers had been removed.

JOE'S REDEMPTION

The auditorium was packed. Banners and balloons were everywhere. You could feel the electricity in the air. Sam, another department leader, tapped Joe on the shoulder. "Hey, Joe! Where's the rest of your team? I can't believe they would miss this," he said.

"They volunteered to man the phones during the event. We were expecting high volume this afternoon, and they were the first to offer to help," Joe replied and then made his way to an open seat and sat down. Looking around, he noticed how people from different departments were all talking, smiling, joking, and sitting together. Even Workforce Management was starting to come around. "What a difference," he thought to himself.

Everything started to change when the new management team arrived. Mary, the former director of customer service, had retired after 15 years of running the center and was replaced by Susan, who had been hired from another company. Among the employees, she was known as "Susan the Shredder." Anything that got in the way of better performance, no matter where it came from, Susan set out to "shred" and replace with a better way.

Even better, she listened. Six months earlier, when Susan first came on board, she set up individual meetings with every department manager, including Joe. Joe could clearly remember how terrified he was. He had no idea what to expect from the meeting. He decided beforehand to just say "yes" and keep his head down. But Susan was not content to let him off that easily. In fact, she was relentless. It was a day he would never forget . . .

Susan opened with some cursory small talk and then said, "Joe, in reviewing your file and talking to Mary, it sounds like at first you were a bit of a rabble rouser. But lately, you have been more of a company man. Why the change?"

Joe's blood pressure spiked. "I think I was being a little aggressive about pushing for some changes," he said after a pause.

"Like what?" she asked.

"Oh, nothing important," Joe replied, staring at his shoes.

"Apparently it was important to you at the time. Come on, Joe, you have a get out of jail free card with me here today. What was your concern? I really want to know."

"It's nothing we can change," Joe muttered.

"With that attitude, we will never get better. I did not take this job so we can remain the joke of the industry. You clearly saw something that was holding us back and wanted to speak out against it. I respect that. But

I can't help if I don't know what it was. I need to know what was on your mind."

Joe was trapped. He had to come up with something fast. "Well, I was a little concerned about one of my reps being put on a performance plan. But in all fairness, he had low quality assurance scores."

"So why were you concerned?" she probed.

A little of the old spark fired up, and before Joe knew what he was doing, he blurted out, "He was the best rep in my department."

"Get me his file," she said.

"OK, I will have it on your desk before I leave," Joe said, hoping she would forget.

"No, I mean get me his file now, please."

Joe got up and headed over to his office, feeling dizzy. His hands were shaking slightly as he dug through his files. "You are on thin ice, my friend," he thought to himself. After finding the file, he returned to Susan's office and handed it to her.

Susan opened the file and started paging through the records, the discipline report, past QA rating sheets, and a whole stack of customer compliment letters.

"I recognize one of these customers," she said, picking up one of the letters. "They used to be one of our largest clients. It says here that they considered this rep to be a part of their team and that he was always willing to go the extra mile to help keep their business. So what was the problem?"

"He didn't always say the scripted closing accurately at the end of the call, despite several coaching attempts, so he was put on a performance plan," Joe replied.

"What happened then?" she asked.

"He quit."

Susan stared at Joe for a full minute. He could feel his skin crawl. "Do you think we did the right thing?" she finally asked.

"Well," Joe replied, "policy stated that . . ."

"Forget policy," Susan interrupted. "Do *you* think we did the right thing? I want your honest opinion, not what the book says. Whatever you say is just between you and me."

Joe looked back at Susan, unsure where this was going. "No, we did the wrong thing."

That's it, Joe thought, you finally did it. Time to pack up your office. You just can't keep your big mouth shut. Joe braced himself. But the axe didn't come.

"Well, no kidding!" Susan shouted. "That's what's wrong with this company. We think that following some process is actually the outcome. Customers loved this guy! We should have been learning how he talked to customers to teach others, instead of forcing some insipid phrases. What in the world were we thinking? Losing this guy cost us one of our best customers!" Susan threw the file back down on the desk.

Joe was shocked. He didn't know what to think. He had not dared to hope things could be better for so long that he wasn't sure what to say.

"Joe, what was your idea back then?" Susan asked him. "Be honest with me."

"It wasn't anything that would have flown," he replied cautiously.

"Try me. According to your interview, you are 'a highly creative and energetic person with significant strategic ability.' I want to hear from that person what he thinks."

Joe paused. This did not feel like a trap. She seemed to genuinely want to know. Finally Joe opened up. "Well to be honest, some parts of our QA process are really good, but other parts are too focused on phrases and checking boxes. It punishes reps who try to adapt to the situation even if they end up saving a customer. We should keep the pieces of the process that check for things like accuracy and compliance with legal requirements, but use customer feedback and actual spending for the rest. If someone helps to build a client's business with us, they should be rewarded."

Susan looked Joe squarely in the eye. "I could not agree with you more. I think our entire performance management process needs to be overhauled. In fact, I am forming a committee to redesign, starting from scratch, how we evaluate our reps. I want you to be part of that team. We need someone like you to help make certain that what we build reflects what it is really like out there. What do you say?"

Joe was speechless. "I . . . I would love to. But I just don't know if I have time."

"Don't worry about that. I got an earful from a few of your peers about all the reports you guys are hit with and how little time you are allowed to spend with your team. That's going to change as well."

And that was just the beginning. Susan, with the help of Joe and others, set about changing or eliminating — one by one — whatever obstacles, barriers, and bureaucratic time killers she found. She did not always agree with Joe's ideas, but she always gave a reason why. Some changes worked better than others, but most made things at least a little bit better. There was still a lot of work to do — finding a more effective way to handle spikes in call volume, developing a better shift-bidding process, working more closely with the rest of the organization to prevent the problems customers were having in the first place — but they had made an incredible amount of progress.

And customers noticed. Repeat business was up, attrition was down, and the company's service ranking skyrocketed. For the first time anyone could remember, the CEO also noticed and had planned today's celebration. The crowd broke into applause as he walked to the podium. "So, does anyone know what we're here to celebrate?" he asked. Everyone cheered. The noise was deafening.

"We are here to celebrate the spirit, dedication, and hard work of each and every one of you. Thanks to you, our sales are up, and we have improved our service to the point where we've gone from dead last to right behind the market leader."

That got a standing ovation.

"Is that good enough?" he asked the crowd.

"*NO!*" everyone replied in unison.

"Are we going to settle for *second place?*"

"*NO!*" came the reply again.

"Ladies and gentleman, Susan has told me that all of the credit for this remarkable transformation goes to each of you, 100%. All of the innovation and ideas could not have happened without your creativity and inspired work. But this is just the beginning. We are going to build an entirely new campaign focused on our world-class service delivery. It's going to become the foundation of our brand. And whether or not it works is entirely up to all of us.

"Passionate customers are created by passionate employees. When you answer that call, each one of you is at that moment and to that customer everything that our company stands for. That's a huge responsibility. We have come this far. If we keep up the momentum and stay focused, we *will* win."

The crowd roared.

"Bring it on," Joe thought to himself. "There's nothing our team can't handle."

ACKNOWLEDGEMENTS

There have been many whose brilliance, insight, and encouragement have been critically important in the creation of this work. While there are too many to mention here, I would like to give a special thanks to a few without whose support this book would not have been possible.

Daniel Kahneman, whose generosity, advice, support, insight, and groundbreaking work helped to lay the foundation of the theory behind identifying and removing barriers.

Shane Lopez, whose work on hope and courage helped to show the path to overcoming the fear that plagues organizations everywhere.

Jim Clifton, Chairman and CEO of Gallup, for his faith and encouragement in the power of barrier busting.

Chris Stewart, for providing a crazy idea over dinner on a cold night in December.

Jennifer Robison, whose talents as an editor and research skills made this a much better book than I could have created alone.

The leadership of Gallup Press — Larry Emond, Piotrek Juszkiewicz, and Geoff Brewer — for their advice, support, and guidance.

Martha Jane Power, Trista Kunce, and Kelly Henry for their superb editing, proofing, and fact checking; Samantha Allemang, for her sharp design; and Julie Lamski, Lisa Morock, and Kelly Slater for excellent management of their teams and publishing processes.

And most of all, my wife and son, who inspire me every day to do my own small part to help create a world where every man, woman, and child can reach their full God-given potential, without having to worry that their hopes and dreams will be destroyed by the fears of others.

REFERENCES

The majority of quotes and examples in this book are taken directly from the Barrier Analysis work conducted by Gallup Consulting between 2002 and 2009. These studies were conducted on behalf of a number of organizations representing different industries, functions, levels, and job types.

Anderson, R.C., & White, R. (2009). *Confessions of a radical industrialist: Profits, people, purpose — doing business by respecting the earth.* New York: St. Martin's.

Babcock, L., & Loewenstein, G. (2004). Explaining bargaining impasse: The role of self-serving biases. In C.F. Camerer, G. Loewenstein, & M. Rabin (Eds.), *Advances in behavioral economics* (pp. 326-43). New York: Sage.

Buckingham, M., & Coffman, C. (1999). *First, break all the rules: What the world's greatest managers do differently.* New York: Simon and Schuster.

Cannon, W.B. (1922). *Bodily changes in pain, hunger, fear and rage: An account of recent researches into the function of emotional excitement.* New York: Appleton.

Carter, A. (2009, July 23). "Lehman Brothers: Wall Street's Titanic" [Electronic version]. *Bloomberg Businessweek.*

Clifton, D.O., & Nelson, P. (1992). *Soar with your strengths.* New York: Dell.

CNN.com. (February 6, 1985). *State of the union address.* Retrieved February 7, 2011, from http://www.cnn.com/SPECIALS/2004/reagan/stories/speech.archive/state.of.union2.html

Fleming, J.H., Coffman, C., & Harter, J.K. (July-August 2005). Manage your Human Sigma. *Harvard Business Review, 83*(7), 106-114.

Gallup Panel, based on 2,634 telephone interviews with national adults, aged 18 and older, conducted January 2007. For results based on this sample, one can say with 95% confidence that the margin of error is ±1.9 percentage points.

Gartner.com. (2010, July). *Gartner says worldwide PC shipments increased 21 percent in second quarter of 2010.* Retrieved February 11, 2011, from http://www.gartner.com/it/page.jsp?id=1401136

Gerstner, L.V., Jr. (2002). *Who says elephants can't dance?: Leading a great enterprise through dramatic change.* New York: Collins Business.

Girard, B. (2009). *The Google way: How one company is revolutionizing management as we know it.* San Francisco: No Starch.

Gongloff, M. (2002, June 28). "The prosperous '90s – a hoax?" *CNN Money.* Retrieved February 12, 2011, from http://money.cnn.com/2002/06/28/news/economy/90s_mirage/index.htm

Harter, J.K., Schmidt, F.L., Killham, E.A., & Agrawal, S. (2009, August). $Q^{12®}$ *meta-analysis: The relationship between engagement at work and organizational outcomes.* Omaha, NE: Gallup.

Jones, L.V. (1997). L.L. Thurstone's vision of psychology as a quantitative rational science. In G.A. Kimble & M. Wertheimer (Eds.), *Portraits of pioneers in psychology: Vol. III.* (pp. 85-102). Washington, DC: American Psychological Association.

Kahneman, D., Knetsch, J.L., & Thaler, R.H. (1990). Experimental tests of the endowment effect and the Coase theorem. *The Journal of Political Economy, 98*(6), 1325-48.

Kahneman, D., & Tversky, A. (1979). Prospect theory: An analysis of decision under risk. *Econometrica, 47*(2), 263-91.

Kahneman, D., & Tversky, A. (1984). Choices, values, and frames. *American Psychologist, 39*(4), 341-50.

Lenovo.com. (n.d.). *Company history.* Retrieved February 11, 2011, from http://www.lenovo.com/lenovo/us/en/history.html

Levs, J. (2008, November 19). "Big three auto CEOs flew private jets to ask for taxpayer money." *CNN U.S.* Retrieved February 15, 2011, from http://articles.cnn.com/2008-11-19/us/autos.ceo.jets_1_private-jets-auto-industry-test-vote?_s=PM:US

Marriott.com. (n.d.). *Celebrity Treatment.* Retrieved February 21, 2011, from http://www.marriott.com/Images/CorporateInformation/StoriesOfExcellence/Story%20pdf/AlbertSmith.pdf

McDonald, L.G., & Robinson, P. (2009). *A colossal failure of common sense: The inside story of the collapse of Lehman Brothers.* New York: Crown Business.

McLean, B., & Elkind, P. (2003). *The smartest guys in the room: The amazing rise and scandalous fall of Enron.* New York: Portfolio.

Moore, H.N. (2008, September 12). "Lehman employees and the Wall Street compensation model." *Fortune.* Retrieved February 12, 2011, from http://blogs.wsj.com/deals/2008/09/12/lehman-employees-and-the-wall-street-compensation-model/tab/article/

Northhall, G.F. (1892). *English folk-rhymes: A collection of traditional verses relating to places and persons, customs, superstitions, etc.* London: Kegan Paul, Trench, and Trubner.

NPR.org. (July 21, 2009). *Ex-insider's book details Lehman Brothers collapse.* Retrieved February 12, 2011, from http://www.npr.org/templates/story/story.php?storyId=106760200

Rate, C.R. (2008). What is courage? A search for meaning (Doctoral dissertation, Yale University, 2007). *Dissertation Abstracts International, 68,* 77.

Reingold, J. (2009, July 20). "An inside tale of Lehman Brothers' downfall" [Electronic version]. *Fortune.*

Rieger, T. (2008). *Balancing empowerment and accountability.* Omaha, NE: Gallup.

Rieger, T., & Kamins, C. (2006, December 14). Why you're failing to engage customers. *Gallup Management Journal.* Retrieved February 7, 2011, from http://gmj.gallup.com/content/25711/Why-Youre-Failing-Engage-Customers.aspx

Robison, J. (2010, February 11). Saving Campbell Soup Company. *Gallup Management Journal.* Retrieved February 14, 2011, from http://gmj.gallup.com/content/125687/saving-campbell-soup-company.aspx#1

Robison, J. (2010, March 4). When Campbell was in the soup. *Gallup Management Journal.* Retrieved February 14, 2011, from http://gmj.gallup.com/content/126278/campbell-soup.aspx#1

Rosner, B. (2005, March 2). "Workplace best and worst: Bad policy: readers respond with the worst company policies they've ever experienced." *ABCNews.com.* Retrieved February 14, 2011, from http://abcnews.go.com/Business/WorkplaceBestWorst/story?id=541596

Schuman, M. (2010, May 10). "Lenovo's legend returns" [Electronic version]. *Time.*

Siy, A., & Kunkel, D. (2007). *Sneeze!* Watertown, MA: Charlesbridge.

Snopes.com. (n.d.). *Bless You!* Retrieved February 28, 2011, from http://www.snopes.com/language/phrases/blessyou.asp

Snyder, C.R., & Lopez, S.J. (2006). *Positive psychology: The scientific and practical explorations of human strengths.* Thousand Oaks, CA: SAGE.

Southwest.com. (n.d.). *About Southwest.* Retrieved February 14, 2011, from http://www.southwest.com/html/about-southwest/index.html

Strahilevitz, M.A., & Loewenstein, G. (1998). The effect of ownership history on the valuation of objects. *Journal of Consumer Research, 25*(3), 276-89.

Tilman, L.M. (2009, February 5). "Survival of the (financially) fittest: Evolutionary pressures and economic fate." *Forbes.com.* Retrieved February 21, 2011, from http://www.forbes.com/2009/02/05/financial-darwinism-recession-opinions-darwin09_0205_leo_tilman.html

Tully, S. (2008, September 21). "The end of Wall Street" [Electronic version]. *Fortune.*

Turner, J. (2010, March 1). "Lost in Penn Station: Why are the signs at the nation's busiest train hub so confusing?" *Slate.com.* Retrieved February 14, 2011, from http://www.slate.com/id/2246104/

Tversky, A., & Kahneman, D. (1981). The framing of decisions and the psychology of choice. *Science, 211*(4481), 453-58.

Twain, M. (1986). *Pudd'nhead Wilson and those extraordinary twins.* New York: Penguin.

Vitullo-Martin, J., & Moskin, J.R. (Eds.). (1993). *The executive's book of quotations.* New York: Oxford University Press.

Wright, J.P. (1979). *On a clear day you can see General Motors: John Z. De Lorean's look inside the automotive giant.* New York: Avon.

About the Author

Tom Rieger pioneered the study and science of organizational barriers and is an expert in applying behavioral economic principles to help understand how large complex systems self-destruct. Through this work, he has become a recognized leader in developing methods and frameworks to identify and remove barriers to success for societies and companies. He regularly consults for a variety of organizations across multiple industries and sectors. In 1994, Rieger joined Gallup, where he is the leader and chief architect of Gallup's worldwide consulting efforts regarding barriers. He is also an expert in international research and polling methods as well as in developing and applying statistical models to a variety of complex organizational issues.

Prior to joining Gallup, Rieger designed and ran a global customer measurement program for a Fortune 100 company and worked with predictive models for new brands and strategies. He received a Master of Science degree in Industrial Administration from Carnegie Mellon University's Tepper School of Business in 1986 and currently resides in Southern California.

Gallup Press exists to educate and inform the people who govern, manage, teach, and lead the world's six billion citizens. Each book meets Gallup's requirements of integrity, trust, and independence and is based on Gallup-approved science and research.